FOLLOWING JESUS
WHEN THE CHURCH HAS LOST ITS WAY

MICHAEL J. SUTTON

ISBN: 978-0-6455671-3-7

Published by Hidden Road Publishing

Also available, as part of the Freedom Matters Today
series, written by Michael J. Sutton:

*Freedom from Fascism, A Christian Response to Mass
Formation Psychosis*

Is God on America's Side?

Is Russia Our Enemy?

DEDICATION

To those who love God but cannot accept the hypocrisy of the church, to those who follow Jesus, but refuse to engage in sectarianism, to those who seek faith but will not support the fascists, this book is for you. Don't go to church my friends, follow Jesus instead.

CONTENTS

Acknowledgments   i

1   Return of an Ancient Enemy   1

2   Be Strong in the Lord   6

3   Put on the Full Armor of God   19

4   Our Struggle   42

5   We Do Not Wrestle Against Flesh and Blood   57

6   Is God a Republican?   70

7   Following Jesus When the Church has Lost its Way   83

8   When the Church Gives Up on Christ, it Returns to Fascism   93

ACKNOWLEDGMENTS

To the many American Christian Fascists, who have taken the wonder, beauty, and truth about God and twisted it into the vengeful, sectarian monster of Christian Nationalism, with its whitewashed history, godless ritualism, and Christless religion, this book could not have been written without you. Thank you.

1   RETURN OF AN ANCIENT ENEMY

What does it mean to follow Jesus? Can a person follow Jesus and not attend church? Are you free as a Christian to vote for whomever you want? Can faith and flag go together? Is Christian Nationalism a valid Christian approach to politics? Is America witnessing the rise of the ancient enemy of fascism? Is it the duty of a Christian to oppose the flaming arrows of the Left? Are socially conservative values, Christian values, the only home for Christian political witness? Has the church lost its way?

American Christianity stands at a crossroads. It is in rapid decline, and the choice is no longer between faith and flag but between witness and oblivion. Most in the church will choose oblivion and will laugh all the way to Hell. When Christians give up on God, they always become fascists, and it is no coincidence that the collapse of Christian witness in America is related to the rise of what many call *'Christian Nationalism.'* There is nothing Christian about it. This term is a euphemism like *'collateral damage.'*

Why don't we call it by its real name? Christian Nationalism is fascism. True fascism comes from the church, and it is, in essence, the blending of faith and flag. This has been the curse of the West for over a thousand years, built on the bodies of millions of innocent people murdered by the church, waving their flags, defending their nations, and killing their people. True Christians follow Jesus, counterfeit Christians promote a Christian nation. It is time for everyone to choose, and you need to take a side, either follow Christ or the church, either take up your cross or your sword, either seek God's kingdom or build man's kingdom. Your Christian nation will fall, your moral crusade will collapse, and your kingdoms on earth will crumble. Whether America rises or falls is not the concern of a follower of Christ, all that matters is the freedom, the liberty, and the joy that comes from knowing God and being known by God through the death of Jesus Christ on the cross, where Jesus stood in our place, and died for our sins, so we might be reconciled to God. The rest is background noise. For the fascists who run the church, the good news is a footnote to their Culture War, but for Christians, Christ is everything and the light of Jesus shines even in the darkest places, for all people who seek hope and who want to be free.

There is a war in America. It is not a war over culture or politics, but over life, and I am not talking about abortion. At stake are the eternal souls of over 300 million people, who live in the most powerful nation in the world today. America most certainly is facing huge social, economic, and political problems. It is entirely possible that it will decline, decay, or even fall, but these questions are incidental to the most important question: who is Jesus Christ? Whether a person answered that question today, or 100 years ago, the path for a Christian is the same: follow Jesus. But what does that look like? The factory setting for American Christians is trying to make America a Christian nation, but this is not Christianity.

What is happening in America is not the result of Trump or any political leader. It is the result of political decay, it is driven by the slow, torturous but inevitable demise of democracy, for fascism always emerges when the contradictions of democracy cannot be managed. I never thought at the end of 2022 I would be writing a book on the return of fascism in the West. Something so evil, so malevolent, so destructive, an ideology with a personality more vicious and vindictive than Communism, and more deceitful and devious than Democracy, the ancient enemy has returned. It is not a specter that haunts Europe, it is a disease than infects the world. It is not a challenge to the power of freedom, it is a ravenous spirit that hides behind liberty, consuming all but a paper-thin façade. It has found expression in the decline of representative democracy in the West, the implosion of self-loathing and political cannibalism in America, the backward lurching of Brexit, the xenophobic white supremacy of Australia, and the decadent decline of the old fascist powers of Italy, France, Germany, Spain, and Portugal, along with the long-suppressed fascist nations such as medievalist Poland, and American-run Ukraine.

Sadly, many who claim to follow Jesus have been swept up in this movement, and they sometimes go by the name of Christian Nationalists. Maybe you are one, or maybe you know one. My prayer is that this book can be like a manual for some, a medicine kit for others, and an antidote for the rest. I encourage you to think about America from a Christian perspective, and open the Bible, read, listen, and pray that you might follow Jesus when the church has lost its way. *Freedom Matters Today* looks at freedom from a Christian perspective, but for most people, even looking from any perspective is too fundamentalist. This means the West is probably out of time.

The greater tragedy is not that fascism is on the rise. It always will be when Christians give up on Christ. The fascists will say *'what would Jesus do?'* but the Christian says, *'what did Jesus do.'* There we have the difference between the fascist and the Christian in a nutshell. The fascist is not interested in the actions or the identity of Christ, but for the Christian, that is all that matters, for Jesus Christ is the Way, the Truth, and the Life.

The greatest tragedy is that the twelve disciples of Jesus changed the shape of the entire world, but Christians today make no impact on their society whatsoever. They have their clubhouses, little cults, sanctums, monasteries, and orders, and they stay inside with their polish, scrubbing brush, and *'to-do list,'* and above all, their rules, and they are completely irrelevant. From time to time, another disciple of Jesus comes along, like Uchimura Kanzo, Francis Xavier, or Hudson Taylor, and church people all stand in awe and write books about their life. They wax lyrical about their achievements but have no intention of doing the same.

Everyone in the world should know the gospel of the good news of Jesus Christ by now, but the simple fact remains that the church has opposed the proclamation of the gospel for centuries. The last thing the church wants are for people to follow Jesus. The Dutch came to Java (now Indonesia) over 300 years ago and instead of telling them the good news of Jesus, the Dutch Reformed Church kept the people of that great archipelago in poverty, slavery, and misery. The British came to the continent of Australia, slaughtered the indigenous people, committing genocide and terror for over a century, and forced thousands of those who remained into church education where their culture was beaten out of them, and they learned of the glory of white civilization, and their alleged (and scientifically fraudulent) descent from monkeys.

The best example of the utter failure of Western civilization to proclaim the gospel was that of the Jewel of the Crown, India. The British deindustrialized the nation that was able to successfully compete with the tiny, filthy island we know as England, a nation that had kept the masses in poverty for centuries aided and abetted by a corrupt Church of England and a slavish, hideous, plagiarized version of the Romish rite of the Mass. The British raped India of its resources and minerals did virtually nothing to provide infrastructure, education, or health services, and spent centuries profiteering from the hard work of the Indian people.

The Church of England and other fascists were there not to preach Jesus Christ, but about White Civilization, white values, and the superiority of

British culture, none of which are in the Bible. Even today, fascist organizations like the Church Missionary Society must admit the complete and utter failure of the Indian Mission. In an irony of history lost among the white supremacists that run it today, the Australian branch of the Church of England was an offshoot of the Indian Mission. It has no origins in white England but in Hindu, Muslim, and Sikh India. The origins of the Church of England in Australia are not in England, but in Kolkata, India, in 1825. Tell that to the fascists in the Australian high church with their plumb voices, tailored London suits, church schools, indulgent racism, and tax exemptions. They will probably call it misinformation and fake news, but you can Google it.

Today's church is full of people who will try to recruit you to their club, get you to attend their service, sign your kids up to their kid's program, force your teenagers into their teen groups and youth groups, where they are vulnerable to all kinds of spiritual and physical abuse. This is all designed to build a business to pay a good salary to a large group of people who, if they worked in the private sector, would be fired after one week.

Churches are the most poorly run, idiotic institutions in a capitalist society, they no longer perform any social or class function, are increasingly irrelevant, and yet linger like that other great relic of the feudal age, the monarchy. Pastors, ministers, and priests are the most corrupt class of people in our society, and yet they laugh all the way to the bank with your money, for doing very little. They recruit to keep the church doors open and the clergy class employed, a class as peculiar as the socially dysfunctional people who tend to attend church each Sunday, sit in the same seats, doze off during the sermon, and eat the same stale food for morning tea afterward without complaint, while spreading infectious diseases.

There were no Sunday Schools before the 1780s. The church didn't believe in education for ordinary people then, only for the elites, the wealthy, and the capitalists. For centuries the Church of England supported the misery of the poor, hated them, and resisted all attempts at social reform. None of these Sunday Schools were Christian, they functioned as instruments of the class war, to foster rudimentary education so people could understand the basics of the machinery they were being squashed by as they could work for the rich. These schools were not created to teach about God, but about one's place in society, and for the poor, it was to work in filth and squalor, for a pittance, to build industry and nation. There were no youth groups before 1945, and there were no teenagers either. There were boys and men, or girls and women, and society encouraged people to work as soon as possible.

The corrupt Keynesian welfarism that began in the 1930s fostered the delayed employment system of the youth keeping them leisured and useless for the ten years they might be the most productive, to protect the wages of unions and other industrial associations. The teenage myth helped prop up the American cult of prosperity only made possible by child slavery around the world that made cheap products for American and Western children to live for 21 years before they did anything productive. Churches were happy to provide moral instruction and free childcare which in many cases they did quite well, but they produced generations of apostasy, superficial faith, and indifference. The American teenager could move to Elvis, drink soda pop, and read comics thanks to child slavery around the world.

Along the way, the churches supported every war their governments began, including Vietnam and the War on Terror. They did this for money of course. After all, they didn't believe in the fear of God, but they believed in whipping up the fear of the Communists and then the Muslims and they made a fortune. We are living at the end of this system, and it is in its death throes, though the glossy pamphlets, beautiful websites and videos, and music performances will say otherwise, the post-war Western church system is dead.

Church people will recruit you to join their church, but they don't care about the Saviour. They never talk about him; he means nothing to them. All that matters is your participation in their ritual, your membership in their club, and your money in their bank accounts. Yet, anyone can know the Saviour and they can know him every day, all day, and everywhere because he is the Savior of the world, and no church owns the patent on him. How are we to follow Jesus when the church has lost its way? This is the question this book seeks to answer.

2   BE STRONG IN THE LORD

Freedom from forgetfulness

The greatest failing of the Christian today is forgetfulness. This is the plague of faith. This failing has nothing to do with politics, nor does it have anything to do with sectarian disputes. Christians will argue amongst themselves until the return of Christ, as they hate no one more than each other. It is not that Christians forget their *'Christian heritage.'* It is not that Christians forget their political obligations to force pagans to adopt *'Christian values.'* It is not that Christians forget their economic and political power in society to transform their nation into a *'Christian nation.'*

It is far simpler; it is far more personal, and it is far more relevant to the life of each Christian. Christians simply forget who they are, and they forget who God is. How this is possible, how it happens and how to avoid it are the questions we will ponder for the moment. How can we find freedom from forgetfulness and rediscover who God is and who we are?

It is not easy to remember anything in a society that tries to make you forget. This is our Western world, a society infused with various social drugs all designed to act as a kind of opiate. Marx was wrong about religion being the opiate of the masses. Indoctrination knows no creed. Just look at Covid Hysteria and what some have called *'Mass Formation'* psychosis, the hypnotic delusion of millions to find comfort in a political solution to a public health crisis that never intended to work.

People have been mass indoctrinated. People have been weaponized to hate. People have become vessels of perpetual fear and despair. From Covid, the West pivoted into the Ukraine war which occurred not when Covid vanished, but when the death toll and adverse vaccine reactions

6

rocketed, certainly in Australia. In Australia, at a time when more people die from the disease of Covid even when they are fully vaccinated, society is now almost completely back to normal. Virtually everyone has pivoted to the new threat: Russia.

One of the casualties of Covid Hysteria was the death of public debate. There is now only one side to every argument. During martial law in Australia, questioning vaccine policy, masks, and anything the government announced was seen as a crime and treason. In some places, it still is. Now, there is truth and there is a conspiracy theory, there is the right answer and there is fake news. We live in an age of revived western political fascism. We are witnessing the terminal decline of liberal democracy. This, I have said before is preparation for war. We are now waist-deep now in our war against Russia in Ukraine as the contours and objectives of WW3 are revealed, carefully, and slowly by the West, including Australia. Christian fascists will support WW3 all the way to doomsday.

Fascism means that institutions once proclaiming independence from the state will seek closer ties to the government in public/private partnerships. This is seen no more clearly than in the church. Take American Christianity, a case study of well-advanced Christian Fascism. American Christians like to pretend that their faith is independent of the state, (so-called *'separation of church and state'*) but they live under the shadow of the Supreme Court and charity rules that define their priorities and their financial integrity. They are not free.

Many American Christians are in ecstasy over the Supreme Court ruling on abortion, proclaiming that it is a win for God. Does God need the Supreme Court to accomplish his purposes for humanity? Christian Fascists will say that he does, but they are wrong. The only one God needed to accomplish his purposes was Jesus Christ, who fulfilled his mission so that we can stand before God, free, and our freedom has absolutely nothing to do with the state or what it does, ever.

American Christians have largely forgotten who they are, and they have forgotten who God is. The great contest of history is over. The battle was fought, but it was not in America. The kingdom of God has arrived, and American Christians have, overall, rejected God's kingdom for their own earthly kingdoms of money and political power. They fight to control the state, Congress, and the courts to impose their political kingdom on others because they have given up on God and God's power.

Jesus stood against Diabolos and won. The devil withdrew, regrouped and now he runs politics. We see his handiwork even in this pyrrhic victory of abortion in America. Christians are called instead to:

'Be strong in the Lord and in his mighty power' (Ephesians 6:10).

Since the faith of many American Christians depends entirely on what the government does, it is no surprise that they have forgotten these words of Paul and they have forgotten who God is.

Freedom from weakness

Forgetfulness influences our understanding of ourselves and our understanding of God. Many Christians define their faith in terms of their ability to influence, control and capture political power to sustain their faith or their life of faith. This is Christian fascism, but it is not Christianity. Paul tells his readers in Ephesians 6: 10, *'finally, be strong in the Lord and in his mighty power.'* Christians today have forgotten this imperative, and they have forgotten that the true source of strength is not us but Jesus Christ, our Lord, and we can stand alone in this world if Christ stands with us.

Being a follower of Jesus means that we can leave weakness behind. Indeed, we can experience daily freedom from weakness. Weakness is however our default position. It is our natural inclination. Nowhere do the writers of the New Testament expect that we rise each day with exuberance and joy, able to face the world with stubborn resilience. This is the road to ruin.

We need to rise to face the day in the context of a real relationship with the living God that pulses through our spiritual veins, one that is real, not only invoked on Sunday mornings. Those who talk about special times of consecration and devotion to God as proof of a transformed life set up false expectations for daily experience. Our default position is weakness.

Paul's call for us to *'be strong'* is an imperative in Greek. This means that it is something we need to do, something we need to remind ourselves to do, and something we must do. The Christian life is not automatic. It is life but life in Christ, but it is still life. Christians do not live in the clouds with cherubs and angels, but on earth with filth and sin, chaos and overcrowded schedules, crying children and aching bones, of past problems and current challenges. It is in the everyday life that our faith is both expressed and defined, and Paul tells us to *'be strong.'*

There is also a good word that prefaces the verse and offers us genuine comfort in life. The past is the past. Leave it there. The word before *'be'* is *'finally,' 'from now on,'* or *'henceforth.'* From now on, be strong in the Lord, says Paul. What he means is that it is never too late to begin this wonderful journey with the Lord Jesus Christ. It is easy for Christians to give over their minds, souls, and hearts to the priest, to the church, and to society and expect them to sustain their faith.

Indeed, most Christians expect other humans to sustain their faith, the idiocy of the Mass to sustain their faith, or the Sunday worship to sustain their faith. The only one who can is Christ. He is the only source of strength and power in life. God is the one who sustains his people because he is the one who exerted all his energy in life and death in standing for his people in their place on the cross. How can flesh and blood, troubled with the same afflictions you have, give you strength for the day ahead? Sure, you can be encouraged by others, but they cannot carry you and they can give you no strength. It is only God who gives us the power and strength to carry on.

Weakness is inevitable, but we can have freedom from weakness if we resolve to leave our past forgetfulness behind and *'from now on,'* be strong in the Lord and in his mighty power. Weakness is not a weakness. It is a reminder to those who follow Christ and who have come to rejoice in the Savior who stood in our place, that we need the strength of another, we need the presence of Christ, we need the power of Christ, and we need the privileges of Christ. We rise each day in weakness, but we can resolve to be strong, for we have the choice to be free from weakness and give up forgetfulness.

Christian Fascists will tell you to wait till the Bible Study on Wednesday or the Mass on Friday or the sermon on Sunday because it is then you can get your weekly injection of spiritual power. Tell them to go to hell, because all Christians everywhere can walk each day in the complete, full, power of God, being strong in the Lord.

Freedom from strength

Have you ever felt alone, truly alone? Have you ever felt that there was no one there to support you and no one who cared? Most have. Many experience the clouds of daily melancholy, that fall like mist on the soul, a gentle layer of coldness for the day ahead, and we crave anything that might lift our spirits, be it a ray of sunlight, a kind word, or the fellowship of others. Many never experience it, and many are alone.

Have you ever been to church and been ignored? I have. It happened a lot. It happens to lots of people, most people in fact. It is why churches appoint *'welcome pastors'* so no one else needs to talk to new people and take time away from their social club gatherings. Churches can be dreadfully lonely places because they are not where Christians gather, they are places where people gather who participate in a ritual. Once the ritual is over, their Christianity ends for the week and they become the same selfish, narcissists they were when they entered the church doors an hour before. This is all undermined by Paul's imperative in Ephesians 6: 10:

'Finally, be strong in the Lord and in his mighty power.'

We have reflected upon our forgetfulness and the possibility of being free from weakness by relying on Jesus for our strength. Most people, I dare to say, fall into the category of the previous reflection, beginning a day from a position of weakness. But not all do. Many are strong people. They have a reservoir of internal power; they have an endless supply of natural enthusiasm, and nothing seems to sway them. While many people crave the presence and power of God in their lives, others dare not tip their toes in the water because they have their own strength, their own power, and their own determination.

Relying upon the Lord is a sign of weakness for these Christians because they don't need God in the way others do. These are the *'super Christians,'* those valiant few who stand firm because Christianity is obvious, it is natural, and it makes sense. They are too good for others, they know it all, they have been to Bible College, they have done the required readings for the week, and they look down upon others who talk of faith as something daily, something real, and something complicated.

There is no greater source of spiritual pride than the values of those who march out of seminary every year. They have tasted the heavenly things; they have been infused with years of Bible teaching and they know everything. They are ready to lead, ready to judge, and ready to laugh at the weakness and stupidity of those who were not godly enough to go to seminary. You can easily spot a seminarian graduate online. It is dead easy. They often have a good following, people of like prejudice in the truest meaning of the word. First, they are difficult to understand. They use words that nobody uses, and few understand. They use these sentences and phrases because they think they are still in the lecture hall, and normal people speak that way.

Second, since most are dedicated Christian fascists, they think that everyone in the world understands where they are coming from and what they are saying. To use a colloquial expression, *'they preach to the converted.'* In other words, they are only interested in reaching a tiny group of people who think like them. God forbid if some pagan stumbles onto their page. Most Christian ministers are online to advance their ecclesiastical career, and once they land a good job, their online journey ends.

The third way to spot them is in their sectarian attitudes. They are usually in one camp or the other, and they are keen to point out their political affiliations, whether they are right-wing or left-wing, evangelical, or liberal, pro-Trump or anti-Trump.

To those valiant strong people who do not need to walk with Christ because it is beneath them, after all, they are priests and bishops, I say a few words of chastisement. First, Paul's imperative to *'be strong in the Lord and in his mighty power'* is for you too, not just your congregations. Your strength will run out and when it does you will probably discover you had no faith to begin with. They were all words, bluster, and bravado.

A person of true faith is open to God, open to learning new things, someone who is genuinely humble and is excited to learn from all people not just the educated, and someone who wants to truly communicate to all people the wonder and power of a life transformed by Christ. Second, for the strong, I offer this prayer:

'Lord, this day, teach me something new about you, your world, your people, and me. May I be strong in the Lord, not in my own strength, my own learning, my own past, and my own privileges. I lay them all at your feet and consider them of no importance, no significance save that you found me and rescued me and gave me life, hope, and a future. My strength I lay at the cross and henceforth strive to be strong in you, my Lord Jesus.'

Freedom from loneliness

To those of you who believe our nation is perfect and the greatest in history, I urge you to go to a nursing home and experience for a few moments what many feel every day in their last months and years, unrelenting, mind-numbing, soul-destroying loneliness. I used to visit several every week. The eyes of everyone lit up as I entered the room, not because there was anything special in me, but because another human being had turned up to see them. Even the staff were happy, and they were keen to add me to the program, a program sparse with activities.

Some people were blessed by kind relatives who visited them regularly and I got to know some of them, and they too were happy to see me. The rest had been dumped there by their family to be forgotten. Many had old photos of their children on their walls, but they were old photos, and their families had long since moved on and left them behind.

I left with the certain conviction that the heart of a nation is only as compassionate as the way it treats the vulnerable and I concluded that Australia is a cesspool. This great nation dumps its elderly like trash in the garbage. To the filth who dump their parents in these hellholes I say this:

Friend, visit there one day, this will be your future too, a life of neglect and unbelievable loneliness. What you mete out to others, will be meted out to you, so prepare if you dare, to stare at a wall for hours on end, for loneliness will precede your eternity in hell.

But there is another way, and that is to experience the freedom from the loneliness that comes from knowing God. Uchimura Kanzo wrote his famous autobiography titled *'Alone with God and Me,'* which really was to say that with God, you are never alone, and this is what Paul is saying in Ephesians 6: 10:

'Be strong in the Lord and in his mighty power.'

We are not alone because we can be strong in the Lord and in his mighty power. All of those who follow Jesus need to remind themselves that Christ is present in their lives, in their hearts, and in their very being. He is not waiting for them at church on Sunday to turn up. He never leaves his people. He never leaves them alone. He never leaves them lonely.

It is more than a simple presence with God. Being a Christian means having the strength and power of God in our lives. We cannot be strong in ourselves, but we can be strong in Jesus. He is our source of strength and power. Paul locates the power of God in the person of Christ for us, each day as we follow him. It is a radical and incredible statement. Jesus is not just alive and seated at the right hand of God, but he is personally and presently with us, and this presence is defined by his power.

Paul can say this because he knows this, and true faith can be spread if it is experienced. This is the problem today in the church because now faith is entirely defined by what happens in the Magic Show on Sunday, which is the Mass or the sermon, or the light show. A life of faith, of following Christ is gone, replaced by the stale dead ritualism of Christian fascism. A life of trusting in God, of walking each day in the power of Christ has been replaced by sectarianism or recruitment into the Culture Wars.

Paul tells us to be strong in the Lord because he was. It was a daily reality for him, and it can be a daily reality for us. But we need to understand that we need it, and that takes genuine faith and humility. To be strong in the Lord means that we are not lonely for we have the Lord, and he knows us, and he loves us for he died for us.

Our walk with God must be based on the certainty of our relationship with God which depends on the certainty of the promises of God found in the Lord Jesus Christ. Paul wrote earlier in Ephesians about this in 1: 18-

20 in his prayer for all who follow Jesus:

'I ask that the eyes of your heart may be enlightened, so that you may know the hope of His calling, the riches of His glorious inheritance in the saints, and the surpassing greatness of His power to us who believe. These are in accordance with the working of His mighty strength, which He exerted in Christ when He raised Him from the dead and seated Him at His right hand in the heavenly realms.'

Freedom from despair

A while ago, I fell in love with a particular kind of Chinese tea. It was black tea, and I made a pot each day. Having one pot was not enough and soon one pot became two and even three. This wonderful tea sustained me physically during many of my days working on the blog posts and podcasts for Freedom Matters Today.

Just as people drink tea to sustain themselves, others have more potent draughts. For example, there is the tea of despair, the elixir of desperation, and the tonic of anxiety. They drink from this pot daily, and they are sustained in a state of lingering, unrelenting sadness. They seem to find these tea leaves somewhere, there are many people selling these brands of tea, and they are very popular today.

We live in a world of political deceit, and crisis culture, pivoting from one disaster to the next, and the result, the desired result is despair. It is tragic to see intelligent, educated people believe the utter nonsense of a diet of fake news, despite being quadruple vaccinated, huddling in fear at home, or watch them reduce complex issues such as the war in Ukraine into categories such as *'goodies and baddies.'*

If there ever was a time for the good news of the grace of God found in the Lord Jesus Christ, then it is today. I am not talking about the church or Sunday rituals, I am speaking of a relationship with God and his Son Jesus who came to die for sin, in our place on the cross. It was at the cross where true power was revealed when the Son of God laid aside his divinity and accepted death, and in that death absorbed all the wrath of God for sin, our sin, sin that condemned us, he took it upon himself and where we should have died, he died.

This is the power Paul speaks of in Ephesians. It is about Christ, not about me, it is about Christ, is it not about the church, it is about Christ, it is not about the Culture War. For Paul, to live is Christ and to die is gain (Philippians 1: 21).

We can be strong in the Lord because of what Jesus has done for us in taking away our fear of despair because all despair was taken into him, felt by him, and understood by him. If you feel despair, then know that Jesus did too, and he can tell you about it. Read about his sufferings in Gethsemane (Luke 22: 44). If you feel shocked at betrayal, then know that Jesus did too. Read about his betrayal (Luke 22: 48). If you feel desolation and despair that you have been deserted by all, know that Jesus was too. Read about his sufferings on the cross when the face of God turned away (Mark 15: 34).

Sometimes the Bible presents pictures of our relationship with God. A common one that Jesus uses is of the cross, which is a symbol of death. Being a Christian is simply someone who follows Jesus, and the path of Christ was not an easy one, nor will it be an easy one for all who follow him. Being a Christian means saying goodbye to the easy road and walking where Jesus trod. The early Christians understood this to be the path to martyrdom for so many ended up being killed for the testimony about the risen Lord Jesus. Jesus said in Luke 9: 23:

'Whoever wants to be my disciple must deny themselves and take up their cross daily and follow me.'

Most people when they hear this think: *'I thought being a Christian meant going to church once a week, what is this you say about 'daily' and this thing about the cross? Didn't Jesus die so I don't have to carry anything?'*

We do not carry anything alone because we are with Christ. In fact, we are united to Christ by faith, and we have access to the power of Christ. In Ephesians 1, Paul reminds the followers of Jesus in Ephesus that they truly understand in their hearts and minds that Christ has called them to genuine hope for the future (Ephesians 1: 18), that as followers of Jesus they will inherit all the privileges and blessings of Gods people (Ephesians 1: 18), and that those who believe have God's *'incomparably great power.'* (Ephesians 1: 19). This power Paul tells them and tells us

'...is the same as the mighty strength he exerted when he raised Christ from the dead and seated him at his right hand in the heavenly realms.' (Ephesians 1: 19-20).

Let these words sink in today. Raising the dead is incredible power and this is for all who believe in the risen Lord Jesus.

Freedom from powerlessness

I once knew a minister whose goal was to get *'bums on seats.'* In other words, he was playing a numbers game. I met him years ago when I was a child, who had come to faith in Jesus quite young. I had known many friends who did not seem interested in the good news of God's grace, and even as a child, I knew that persuading people to genuinely come to faith is ultimately God's work, not mine.

After all, I was a child and I was very aware of how kids get set in their ways early, many of their life choices and future paths already largely determined for them in their youth. But for this priest, all that mattered was getting more people in the church door on Sunday. He was going to convert everyone and all they needed to do was sit down, shut up and listen to him. His church flourished and soon there were hundreds of people coming and there was a need for a new building. For him, it was all about the numbers, the bums on seats. Were lives being changed? No, not really. There wasn't much to do in that suburb in those days. Churches fulfilled a need for bored white people. It was a huge social club with free childcare for kids on the weekend and a great source of income for the church.

God doesn't care about numbers or bums on seats. Even in the parable of the lost sheep, there were only 99 that were not lost. He only called 12 disciples. There was only one Paul and one Apollos. None of the New Testament books make much fuss over numbers. We simply do not know how many came to faith in that first generation aside from the examples in the book of Acts

When God acts, he acts decisively because he has true power. God's power changes lives and not only that, remains available for all who follow his Son, the risen Lord Jesus. This Paul makes abundantly clear in his letter to the Ephesians. There is the verse I mentioned yesterday that Paul wants his readers to know:

'...his incomparably great power for us who believe. That power is the same as the mighty strength he exerted when he raised Christ from the dead and seated him at his right hand in the heavenly realms' (Ephesians 1:19-20).

In Ephesians 3: 7, Paul speaks of his own calling by God:

'I became a servant of this gospel by the gift of God's grace given me through the working of his power.'

In Ephesians 3: 16-17 Paul wants his readers to know that the Spirit of

God brings divine power in their hearts enabling Christ to reside more fully. He says:

> *'I pray that out of his glorious riches he may strengthen you with power through his Spirit in your inner being, so that Christ may dwell in your hearts through faith. And I pray that you, being rooted and established in love.'*

In Ephesians 3: 20, Paul prays that

> *'Now to him who is able to do immeasurably more than all we ask or imagine, according to his power that is at work within us.'*

Paul in Ephesians 1: 19, 3: 7, 3: 16-17, and 3: 20 uses the Greek word dynamos where we get the words like dynamite or dynamic. This means God's divine miraculous power, true power, not something earthly and temporary but something real and lasting and eternal. True power comes from God, and true power resides with those who follow God, and this is not for some, but for all. God's power is for all because of their relationship with God through faith in Jesus Christ.

There is no magic formula to get this power. It is already ours by faith. It already exists in the life of a Christian. This is certainly how Paul understands it. God's power is at work within us (3: 20). God works his power in us in our first encounters with him (3: 7). The power that God used to raise Christ from the dead is ours (1: 19-20).

True Christian power is from God, and it is for all God's people, and it is for all days, good days, and bad days by virtue, or because of our relationship with God. Church, rituals, and traditions have no power. Only God has power. God doesn't want bums on seats, but he wants us out living life, each day, following him, and knowing that God's power sustains us. We need never feel powerless again. Powerlessness vanishes at the foot of the cross when true power is revealed in the work of God to deal with sin, and create hope for the future, because of Jesus.

Freedom from power

Many people today believe that America is the greatest nation in history and deserves to rule the world forever. They have certainly made a good start. In WW2, America firebombed civilian targets in Japan, killing hundreds of thousands of innocent civilians in what was perhaps one of the greatest war crimes in history, alongside the atomic blasts in

Hiroshima and Nagasaki. Bombing the city of Sendai, Nagoya, Kobe, and Osaka involved deliberately targeting civilian buildings, houses, schools, and hospitals. American history books tell us the carpet bombing and atomic blasts were justified and after all, Japan was mad for their love of war, right?

America is also rewriting the war in Europe to airbrush away the critical role of the Soviet Union in destroying Hitler at the same time it supports fascist regimes around the world including Ukraine, Poland, Hungary, and other petty dictatorships and Christian fascist states parading as liberal democracies. The twenty years' war in the Middle East was a series of horrific war crimes but to date, no one has been prosecuted for any of it, the only one really being persecuted is Julian Assange who will spend his life in prison for exposing war crimes allegedly committed by American soldiers in Afghanistan and Iraq.

America is in rapid economic decline due to the rise of China, India, and the rest of the world, but the ruling class in Washington D.C. want to ensure that all competition is emasculated. We are in the early stages of WW3 with Russia and will soon go to war with China. America, like Britain in the nineteenth century, will not tolerate a world run by Asians, nor will they tolerate a world where power is to be shared. They want it all for themselves and want to plunder Russia as well, hoping that trillions of dollars propping up the fascists in Ukraine will lead to civil war in the former Soviet Union.

To knock out China, America, and Europe will need to kill at least 250 million Chinese and perhaps that is the goal. America got away with mass murder in WW2 so perhaps the thinking is they can do it again, especially in the world of mass propaganda. Just notice how quickly the world turned against Russia only a few months after America left Afghanistan after being there 20 years. No one condemned America. Instead, they were given a free pass to send four nations back to the Stone Age.

250 million might be enough to convince China to back down and accept American rule, but this will need a nuclear strike which is entirely possible now. Many in the ruling class are openly touting nuclear war with Russia as an option. Just listen to the American media which are openly calling for Putin's assassination and nuclear war with Russia. Many are saying:

'we can beat them, after all, we are the greatest power in the world, in all of history, there is none like us.'

Now, Trump wants another shot at the White House, to make America great again, again, but his true party slogan is a middle finger pointed at the heavens. He is not alone. This is the slogan of all the parties, no matter their creed. Listen, if you want to be the Messiah, then know this, Messiahs get crucified. If you rise from the dead, maybe you merit some of our time, but fake Messiahs are to be rejected out of hand. As for me, my Lord rose again, and he was innocent of all charges laid against him. Just look at the records of these fake political Messiahs. But look for them, all the Christian fascists lining up to support their new Messiah, and with every step, they turn their backs on Christ and true power.

Paul tells us henceforth to be strong in the Lord and in his mighty power. The word translated power in Ephesians 6:10 is not dynamos but another word, which means more accurately *'strength.'* This is the Greek word *'ischus.'* I think it is sometimes read as *'power'* because 'power' is a generic word that can cover many things. True power is not to be found in Donald Trump or democracy or America, or any nation that thinks they are eternal, but true power is found in the risen Christ. True strength comes from the Son of God. This strength is mighty. This mighty strength means that all who have faith enjoy it, have it, and possess it, all the time.

It is because we forget the privileges of faith that we turn to politics to secure something we cannot have to replace something we never lost. Open your Bible friends, turn off the Culture War, rejoice in the Lord and follow him, the only true, eternal power in the world. Free yourself from fake power and rest in God's strength.

3   PUT ON THE FULL ARMOR OF GOD

Freedom from slavery

A common fear in the world today is a fear of evil, a fear of the supernatural, the fear of the Devil, or Diabolos. The church in the West and especially Christian Fascism has often enlisted fear of the devil to promote their methodology, which is to take our attention away from Jesus Christ and focus it on restoring what they see as Christian values, Christian heritage, and a Christian nation. Christian Fascism is what many call Christian Nationalism, but it is a broader disease afflicting Christian witness, especially in the West. To be a Christian is not to go to church on Sunday, but to have a relationship with God, and as far as nations are concerned, God has no favorites, nor can he be recruited into our petty Culture War. Christians become fascists when they lose their belief in God's kingdom and seek the build a kingdom in their image on earth. In the previous chapter, we pondered Ephesians 6:10, where Paul wrote:

from now on, be strong in the Lord Jesus and in his mighty strength.'

This chapter looks at a much misunderstood and misapplied verse in the New Testament about how Christians are to live in this world without fear. Christians are to be free people, living in the freedom that comes from knowing Jesus Christ, not cowering in fear, trembling, and terror at the world. Jesus says in John 8: 36:

'For if the Son of Man shall set you free, then you shall be free indeed.'

Jesus is true to his word. True freedom is the goal of God's salvation found in Jesus Christ.

My hope is that this book will encourage you to turn to the Bible, open it, and read it. Don't just take my word for it, go to the passages, and verses I am examining and read them for yourselves. Don't listen to the Church, read the Bible instead. You will be surprised, challenged, and hopefully emboldened to live a confident life of faith instead of a dead weekly ritual. The text of the Bible is not the preface to the church ritual, it is not the sideshow to the main event, it is God speaking to us today.

We are considering freedom from slavery, for that is indeed what happens for all who come to faith. There is true freedom from the oppressiveness of a life of slavery. A slave has no choice. A slave must do what they are told. There are no options for a slave. For a person who has come to faith, the choice comes into one's life for the first time. The only freedom one had when one lived in Satan's kingdom, was being blind to the things of God. When the light of the good news of God's grace shone on our hearts, we were set free from the power of Satan to God, and we were delivered from darkness to light (Acts 26).

In turning to God through faith (not baptism, for baptism with water changes nothing), a person moves from bondage to a struggle, from utter defeat to conflict, from a life of spiritual misery to a daily walk with God, from a life of powerlessness to a life lived in God's power. It is a life where choices can be made. Paul gives us an example of this choice in Ephesians 6: 11:

'Put on the whole armor of God so that you can make your stand against the Devil's schemes.'

We see clearly in this verse many things for Paul is very clear in his writing. Today we see is that we have a choice. The time of slavery is over. We are not forced to put on the armor of God, we are not forced into the life of defending ourselves against the Devil's schemes, we are not without freedom in deciding to make a stand. Many Christians, even those who think themselves to be intellectual and intelligent are deeply troubled with Paul's writings on the supernatural. This is rather odd, and it is odd because to be a Christian presupposes a supernatural world, as faith in God implies a belief in someone that one cannot see, that believing in Christ implies a belief in something that is not scientifically possible, that is a person rose from the dead.

During Covid Hysteria, many churches denied the supernatural and apostatized by insisting that we *'follow the science,'* and ignore conspiracy theories such as the idea that people could get Covid after being vaccinated. We know now that science tells us something quite different, but maybe someone should remind Christian Fascists that to be a Christian means accepting a supernatural world.

Paul is writing to his readers to equip them with everything they need to live a life as followers of Jesus Christ. He wishes to help them, aid them, and support them, to give them the skills, ways, and attitudes necessary to face each day as a Christian. When Paul says to *'put on'* the armor of God, he is encouraging them to do so. He is urging them to do so. It is an imperative. It is not *'if you like,'* or *'if you have time,'* or *'you can if you want,'* but he is urging them to do so. It is the image of clothing oneself with something. It comes from the Greek word *'enduo'* which means *'to clothe,'* and it means having this clothing settle onto a person so that they can wear it and it becomes theirs.

A contemporary understanding might be *'wear it properly,'* or *'this armor fits.'* David when he went out to battle Goliath the giant was given armor by Saul that didn't fit him, so he had to take it off. This armor fits. It fits all people of faith. It is a *'one size fits all'* and all are required to *'put on'* the armor of God. This is a comforting thought for all Christians are in the same boat, as it were, there is no hierarchy in God's kingdom, all are one in Christ, there is no class, there are no special people, and those who refuse to wear the armor or believe themselves too good to wear it, or believe that this is only for weak Christians who believe in the supernatural, will face Diabolos alone, and he will most certainly destroy them.

Christ stood for us that we do not need to stand alone, and the Christian is never alone for they have passed from death to life and this life is with the Son, an eternal life where our relationship with God is never revoked. But I cannot for the life of me understand the reasoning behind the *'reluctant evangelical'* whose spiritual life must be as thin as rice paper, whose prayers are as short as a limerick, and whose diet is the fear of their rich, smart friends. The Bible is not good enough for them, as they are studied philosophy and they hedge their bets, and qualify their positions, and they are always looking over their shoulders hoping that their atheist comrades do not see them praying or speaking of Paul too highly.

To these people I say this: have your rice-paper-thin Christian life. You will be cut down in life and ruined because you did not *'put on'* the armor of God. Your whitened bones scorched in the sun will be a lesson to all who pass by, that life is real and at the end of the day, you need to make a choice whom you will worship, your friends, or God, your career, or Christ, money, or eternal life. Put on the armor of God and stand, or leave it off, face Diabolos alone, and lose. A Christian is free to choose. Paul urges us to put on the armor of God so we can make a stand against the Devil's schemes. Clothe yourselves with God's armor.

Freedom from defenselessness

At the time of writing, WW3 begun as the West, led by America, is at war with Russia, defending the puppet regime of Ukraine with more military and financial assistance in less than 6 months than in living memory. The military build-up began in 2014 when Ukraine deceitfully signed the Minsk Agreements with Russia but began bolstering its military infrastructure with Western aid. This *'arming of Ukraine'* caused the war and ensures that it will continue.

The weapons of war today are as horrific as they are ingenious. One could write for hundreds of pages on the types of weapons that have been invented, and the ways of killing that have been devised. There are only a handful of global weapons manufacturers today and they make most of the bombs, missiles, and weapons used in all the conflicts around the world. They compete and collude to devise the best and most technological ways to end human life. Business is booming now and the ones to be affected will be the innocent civilians who have no choice but to suffer. This is all a far cry from the rather ancient and romantic image created by Paul in Ephesians 6 of a person wearing armour and carrying a sword. He writes in Ephesians 6:11 that

'Put on the whole armor of God so that you can make your stand against the Devil's schemes.'

The armor of 2,000 years ago would be inadequate today. A soldier in such armor would be blown to pieces in a war today and that could be done from hundreds of miles away, even if they lived underground. I don't see the point in upgrading Paul's image to modern life, as some have done, for there is no need to glorify war any more than it is glorified already today. War is horrible. War is evil. War is a sin against God, and that is all war.

But it is interesting that Paul chooses body armor and that he chooses an individual soldier rather than a group because he is speaking of a person of faith and their decision to fight. Many have recoiled at the idea of individual spiritual war and argued that Paul is speaking to Christians assembled, but why would he not use an image to convey that? There is no evidence in the text that Paul is speaking to Christians assembled, or to a group. He could have used the image of a Roman regiment huddled together, as everyone would have known the reference. Few people would not have seen the Romans in battle at some point or heard of their many strategies for repelling attack. He also doesn't use the image of a Roman soldier at all and so there is no point trying to educate people on the finer points of Roman armor.

There is no reason why he would have used Rome as a reference point since Rome was the invader and the conqueror and it would have been offensive to many of his readers for Paul to allude to war using the Roman invaders as an example of Christian faithfulness. No, his image is a relatively simple one, that of a man wearing body armor and carrying a sword, an image that would have been familiar to all people of that day.

The most basic reason for wearing armor and carrying a sword is to enable the wearer to prepare for battle, and in that battle, to defend themselves against attack. These days, people do not wear armor or carry swords unless they are going to a re-enactment or a festival, but people in the days of Jesus wore such armor for battle. The fact that Paul likens the spiritual life or the life of a Christian to that of a war should make us take notice immediately.

This is a shock for two reasons. The first is that we are often told, especially by evangelical Christians that the war is over, and we are in a mopping-up operation against the Devil, that he was soundly defeated and that he no longer has any power. The second shock is that the Christian life is likened to a war, as wars are horrible things, and it is a strange way to talk about a life that is lived in the light, as war is often associated with darkness and death.

First, Paul is telling his readers that the Christian life is combative, a struggle, a fight, a conflict, and that is quite consistent with what Jesus said in the Gospels. Paul is simply restating to his readers the same message that Jesus gave about counting the cost and carrying the cross. In Luke 9: 23, for example, Jesus says,

'Then he said to them all: "Whoever wants to be my disciple must deny themselves and take up their cross daily and follow me.'

The image of the cross would have meant martyrdom to many of the readers of the Gospels for that was what Jesus was speaking of a life of dying to self and living to God.

Second Paul is not lying to his readers about the costs, difficulties, and challenges of being a follower of Jesus. He is not like many priests, pastors, and ministers today who make lying for a living their code of practice, who hide the truth of the Gospel from people to take their money each week leading them on with false promises. Paul tells it as it is. Christians need to put on spiritual armor. Christians need to fight. Christians need to be ready. Does not Jesus also say:

'Watch and pray so that you do not fall into temptation?' (Matthew 26: 41, Luke 21: 36).

Many evangelicals present a false image of the Christian life by either painting a life of prosperity for Christians or dismissing spiritual realities. Some argue that there is no spiritual conflict because, at the cross, Satan was destroyed. Some argue that being a Christian is a ticket to the good life, a life of victorious Christian living, of prosperity, and hope. Temptation ruins the first argument and life wreck the second with the Christian who has been lied to by their church floundering on the rocks of despair and misery. Many never rise again, and few return to a life of confident faith.

If only they opened their Bibles in the first place and did not listen to the church. If only they turned to Paul's letter to the Ephesians and read what he said about being ready in the battle against spiritual realities. If only they dismissed the smooth-talking of the used-car salesmen in the church with their false promises of an easy life and turned the pages of the Bible to see that following Jesus is not easy. Jesus says in John 15: 20:

'Remember what I told you: 'A servant is not greater than his master.' If they persecuted me, they will persecute you also. If they obeyed my teaching, they will obey yours also.'

It was fascinating in Covid Hysteria to see many of the great evangelical preachers accept covid passports to churches, or church closures or whatever they needed to do to support the state, all out of a desire to avoid persecution. Many of them were prepared to throw away a lifetime of Bible teaching at the first sign of actual persecution from the state.

In other words, the good news of God's grace was only a message for the days of wealth and plenty and good times. When trouble came, they gave it all up. They were not ready to fight, they did not have their armor on, and they were too Western to prepare for spiritual battle. They had grown fat and lazy and corrupt in the West and lost sight of God. They closed their churches when the coronavirus was beginning and opened when it got worse.

Look at these hypocrites in the Australian church. Tens of thousands of people have covid now, the death rate is skyrocketing, and yet they all opened their churches again. To avoid spiritual war, they closed their churches and closed their Bibles. For them, the state is their friend, and they long to revive Christian values in society as good fascists, and they laugh at Paul and call him a fanatic and close their Bibles and lie to their congregations about God. Good Christian Fascists love Moses and the Law and ignore the grace and mercy of Jesus.

Paul tells us to put on the whole armor of God so we might defend ourselves, which is the point of putting on armor. The threats are real. Following Jesus is not easy. We must be prepared. If you don't put it on, you will fall like the Western Church did during the pandemic. They thought they were too good to put on God's armor and look what happened to them.

Freedom from vulnerability

One of the most obvious things about the vaccines for Covid is that they don't work. They do not protect you from the virus they are meant to protect you from. You get injected and you are told to avoid people if they do not have the injection, but why? Surely you can be around them because you have immunity from the disease, right? We were told originally that once injected with the vaccines then you will not get Covid because you will be immune. No one says that anyone. Now, you can catch covid again, be hospitalized and die from it. Many have. Many have been injected four times and are still getting Covid. These vaccines are probably among the worst vaccines ever created. I know one person who has been injected four times but at some point, contracted Long Covid. Despite this, they still say that they would be worse off if they were not vaccinated. This is self-delusion. Governments even changed the definition of vaccination to cover up this massive political fraud. Despite the science, many people are still completely convinced that they need to be injected with boosters every few months for the rest of their lives, as they huddle at home, too scared to be with their friends and families.

There is no point putting on armor if it doesn't protect you. There is no point in boasting about invulnerability if you remain vulnerable. Paul would not use the image of the vaccine as it would not convey the message he is trying to get across. No one would ever get converted. Paul's message is that God's armor gives us freedom from vulnerability. Paul tells the Ephesians in 6: 11,

'to put on the whole armor of God so that you will be able to stand against the Devil's schemes.'

Paul is telling us to put on this armor, these weapons of faith, to stand against the schemes of the Devil. But it is not only part of the armor, or half of it, or what you need on any given day, but the whole armor of God. We need to be completely defended to completely defend. There can be no hidden gaps or weaknesses, so we are overcome. There is no Achilles

Heel in the armor of God.

Achilles was the great Greek hero. To ensure his invulnerability, his mother took him as a baby to the river Styx and dipped him in the water, protecting all of him from harm except for his ankle where she held him. He ended up being killed by a poisoned arrow that struck him in the heel. We use the term Achilles Heel to refer to a weakness a person may have in life that will eventually bring them down even if they are strong in other areas. In God's kingdom, God's people are protected by God's armor, and it is complete armor. He does not leave us vulnerable.

The word to describe the armor of God is often translated as complete, or full armor. It comes from the Greek word 'panoplia' which is where we get our word panoply. Panoply means originally a complete set of armor. This makes sense from God's perspective. God's salvation is not half-finished, it is not like us, it is not unfinished, or in draft form, or a work in progress, or stages uncompleted, nor does it need to be fixed by us or adjusted for climate, class, or culture. As Paul says in Galatians 3: 28, there is neither Jew nor Greek, male, or female, slave or free, but we are all one in Christ. God's salvation is complete. It is not unfinished. John wrote in John 17: 3:

'Now this is eternal life: that they know you, the only true God, and Jesus Christ, whom you have sent.'

In the same way, God's protection of his people is complete. If we put on the armor of God, then our protection is assured, our defense is certain, and our position is guaranteed. This is not arrogant self-confidence, but a reflection of the armor provided by God. This armor has no weaknesses, it has no chinks, there is no weakness there is no question over its power and efficacy to do the job. This is a great comfort for the soldier in battle, that they can defend themselves against their enemy and do so with the armor provided to them. Soldiers who go into battle with the wrong armor, the wrong weapons, or the wrong tools end up dead. Even the best soldier needs to be protected.

God provides us with his armor because we need to be defended against the Devil's schemes. He would not offer it to us if we did not need it. God is not a time waster. He knows life is precious. His Son died for life and for us so we might have life. God knows life is meant to be enjoyed. His Son said that he has come that we might have life and have it to the full (John 10:10). God knows life is difficult and so he asks us not to be anxious but to pray about everything (Phil. 4: 6-7).

God's armor is God's way of ensuring invulnerability in the life of Christians as they seek to follow Jesus each day. This is not about going to church on Sunday. There is no protection there. Churches do not protect anyone from the Devil's schemes. The old superstition that the church building was consecrated ground or holy ground is simply an awful medieval superstition.

The Devil has taken up residence in many churches, he is welcome there, after all, the language of many churches is one of slander and gossip. In fact, gathering with other believers is not included as part of the armor of God. God's armor is not about participating in a ritual once a week, or once a day. It is not even an external thing. It is not something you do at church, or do often at church, but it is something more intimate, deeper, and more life-changing than that.

Paul uses the word *'clothing yourself'* with the armor of God, which is what we usually translate as *'putting on.'* The word that Paul uses here is a word he uses elsewhere to describe the new life we have in Jesus Christ. The armor is for those who have faith in Christ. For those who were well-versed in Paul, his use of the phrase *'putting on,'* is about the choice of a Christian but it is also a reflection of the new life we have because of coming to faith.

In the Gospels, the term *'put on'* is usually reserved for the putting on of clothes (see for example Matthew 6: 25, Mark 6:9, Luke 12: 22). It is a verb, an action word, of doing something. This act of putting on clothes means you are prepared for the day ahead, for social interaction, and for doing the day what you need to do. It is a simple act. It is a normal act. This is the term Paul uses to describe the change that occurs because of a person coming to faith in Christ. As a result of turning to God through faith in Christ, Paul says, one must put on new clothes reflecting the new position we have in Christ, and discard the clothes that no longer fit, or are no longer appropriate for our position.

How does the New Testament describe this *'putting on'*? The parable of the wedding banquet is one such example (Matthew 22) where one of the wedding guests turns up *'not dressed in wedding clothes.'* (Matthew 22: 11), the original is lost in translation, but the implication is that he is not clothed appropriately for the occasion. The same Greek word is used in Luke 24: 49 when Jesus speaks to the disciples gathered at his ascension and he tells them of the arrival of the Holy Spirit. He says:

'I am going to send you what my Father has promised; but stay in the city until you have been clothed with power from on high.'

Most translations use the word *'clothed,'* which does not refer to actual fabric or cloth, but rather the covering or empowering of a person with God's power. Therefore, while the meaning of *'clothed'* or *'being clothed'* has its origins in fabric and cloth, the more common meaning refers to a new beginning, a new start, a new way of life, new priorities.

Therefore, Paul says *'put on the armor of light,'* (Romans 13: 14), *'put on the Lord Jesus,'* (Romans 13: 14), *'put on the new self'* (Ephesians 4: 24), and in this verse *'put on the whole armor of God'* (Ephesians 6: 11). This armor is for a Christian, it comes from God, and it gives us freedom from vulnerability because it is God's armor for all who wear it, as they walk each day following Christ.

Freedom from attack

Every year in the Japanese town of Ako, there is a wonderful parade on December 13 that marks the tragic story of the 47 Ronin. These were 47 samurai who worked for and served the Lord of that town who was forced to commit suicide under mysterious circumstances whilst on a visit to the capital. There was a scandalous incident in the Shogun's palace in Tokyo in 1701 where their Lord drew his sword, which carried the death penalty. Why he drew the sword, and what the real story was has been lost to history, but the 47 samurai waited for two years before they took their violent revenge on the man, they held responsible, decapitated him, and took the head to the grave of their Lord before taking their own lives.

The parade is a spectacular one or certainly was in the days before Covid. I had the privilege of recognizing one of the participants who was a famous actor, and we enjoyed a delightful conversation. He was astonished that I recognized him since he was not in costume, but sometimes, faces are unforgettable.

During that march, there were a group of men, most of them elderly who marched in the most incredible samurai costumes. They all look brand new, they were meticulous and accurate historically, with helmet, breastplate, arm, and leg guards, and all the trimmings. For students of history, they were remarkable recreations. I have seen them march a few times, but what astonished me at first was their ease with walking, because samurai armor is very heavy, and these men were not young.

Then I discovered this was not real armor, it was in fact light cardboard, paper, and fabric. I remember sighing with relief because the march was long, and it was a hot day. No wonder they sauntered through the town like real samurai. They were not dressed for battle. They were not expecting an attack, except an onslaught of tourists with their cameras and admiration.

Soldiers wear armor to protect themselves in battle. Armor provides freedom from attack. God's armor is sufficient to protect God's people from the attacks of the Devil. We can learn much from Paul's imperative in Ephesians 6: 11:

put on the whole armor of God so that you may make your stand against the Devil's schemes.'

We can learn that an attack is expected. Paul does not only mention this attack in Ephesians, so Christians cannot be quick to discount it. Many seem to think that they are untouchable as Christians, that they are impervious to sin, wickedness, or temptation. Jesus was the Son of God and yet he was tempted by Diabolos. Jesus was the Son of Man and yet he was not untouchable, because they tortured and crucified him.

I once met a man who told me that he had never sinned in his life, that he was not capable of sinning, and that he had never done anything wrong in his life. I quickly looked at his wife who said *'well, you should have heard him this morning.'* I have however met many perfectionists in this life, they are people who think that because they are Christians, they are immune from sin, struggling with sin, or falling into sin. Even pagans know this is impossible, so it is a remarkable delusion for those who claim to know God that they live under such self-deception.

These perfectionists love Paul, (even though they ignore him) so let me remind them of what he says. They have apoplexy over Romans 7 so we will pass over it, as I don't want them to die before the next paragraph. In Romans 13: 12-14, Paul writes:

'And do this, understanding the present time: The hour has already come for you to wake up from your slumber, because our salvation is nearer now than when we first believed. The night is nearly over; the day is almost here. So let us put aside the deeds of darkness and put on the armor of light. Let us behave decently, as in the daytime, not in carousing and drunkenness, not in sexual immorality and debauchery, not in dissension and jealousy.'

Paul here tells his readers to *'put on the armor of light,'* which is an imperative, something his readers are called to do to prepare them for battle, and it is strongly implied in these verses that a Christian life is not an automatic one, but one that requires sensible living, waking up from sleep, getting ourselves together, and standing firm against the ways of life that are not appropriate for Christians. It is a battle. It is obvious that it is. Paul doesn't stop there. In his first letter, he uses the same battle imagery. In 1 Thessalonians 5: 7-9, he says:

'For those who sleep, sleep at night, and those who get drunk, get drunk at night. But since we belong to the day, let us be sober, putting on faith and love as a breastplate, and the hope of salvation as a helmet. For God did not appoint us to suffer wrath but to receive salvation through our Lord Jesus Christ.'

Once again, attacks are coming, the battle is real, you are not immune from temptation, and you are not beyond the schemes of evil even though you have come to faith. Give up this crazy perfectionism as Paul reminds them *'let us be sober,'* and he does through faith hope, and love as parts of armor that as Christians we put on to face the days ahead. Life is tough. Even pagans know this, and they don't even know God so take a leaf from their book and if they are trying to be careful in their life and you are not because you think you are too good to worry about the problems of life, then you are in serious trouble.

Paul is under no illusion about the battle of faith, or the fight of faith (1 Timothy 6:12). The Christian life is not a walk in the park, so why would there be no battle? You can contrast the life of Paul with the super stories of the so-called miracle workers of perfectionism in Christian history. Most stories of the *'victorious Christian living'* of Western saints and personalities during the days of imperialism are either creative hagiography or bare-faced lies. I prefer Paul. At least he is honest, and you get the whole story. He writes in 2 Corinthians 6: 3 -13:

'We put no stumbling block in anyone's path, so that our ministry will not be discredited. Rather, as servants of God we commend ourselves in every way: in great endurance; in troubles, hardships and distresses; in beatings, imprisonments and riots; in hard work, sleepless nights and hunger; in purity, understanding, patience and kindness; in the Holy Spirit and in sincere love; in truthful speech and in the power of God; with weapons of righteousness in the right hand and in the left; through glory and dishonour, bad report and good report; genuine, yet regarded as impostors; known, yet regarded as unknown; dying, and yet we live on; beaten, and yet not killed, sorrowful, yet always rejoicing; poor, yet making many rich; having nothing, and yet possessing everything. We have spoken freely to you, Corinthians, and opened wide our hearts to you. We are not withholding our affection from you, but you are withholding yours from us. As a fair exchange—I speak as to my children—open wide your hearts also.'

Horrible, wretched stuff, and no doubt in the muck and the filth of this experience, Paul grew as a person as we all do when faced with such trials.

So, the Christian life is a battle. It requires determination and decisiveness and for all Christians, it requires a decision to be serious in some things and aware of a world that the world denies exists, that of spiritual reality.

Paul is not telling us to go to war against other people or nations, or societies, and our weapons are not real weapons at all, these are just images he uses to describe the spiritual struggle we have in life against our principal foe – Diabolos.

Even in our struggle against others, we are not against them, but against what they say, their arguments, and their positions. They are not our enemy, no matter what they tell you in church. Don't listen to the church, read your Bible instead. Paul writes in 2 Corinthians 10: 3-5:

'For though we live in the world, we do not wage war as the world does. The weapons we fight with are not the weapons of the world. On the contrary, they have divine power to demolish strongholds. We demolish arguments and every pretension that sets itself up against the knowledge of God, and we take captive every thought to make it obedient to Christ.'

Freedom from inferiority

Inferiority is a word that DIY or Do It Yourself experts know quite well. Inferior products plague the market. They can include dodgy screws, faulty hand tools, brooms that snap under pressure, saws with teeth that have no bite, frames that are not up to scratch, drills with no power, and steel that bends with the wind. Inferior tools hamper good workmanship, and inferior products ruin construction. Inferiority seems to be the fastest-growing language in the construction industry.

When I lived in Japan, I visited the ancient city of Matsumoto for it has one of the oldest, most authentic traditional castles in the nation. Most of the old castles were pulled down in the late nineteenth century because the ruling class believed that anything not Western should be destroyed. In the museum near the castle, there is a suit of samurai armor, and the breastplate is the most fascinating and tragic. It is a beautiful piece of armor, well-made and crafted and skilfully constructed. In the middle of the breastplate is however a single bullet hole. It would have killed the wearer of the armor outright. He would have been dead before he hit the ground. Despite its beauty, wonder, and craftsmanship, the suit of armor was inferior and no match for a rifle.

God only gives us the best armor to fight against the schemes of the Devil. We can be sure, that as Christians, we have freedom from inferiority. God gives us the only armor capable of sustaining an attack from Diabolos. It is made by God, it is not hand-made, but God-made, it is divinely made and crafted of the best materials. The armor needed to repel spiritual attacks could not be made by us, we would not even know how to do it, the skills have long been lost to humans since the very beginning of creation. Paul is convinced when he tells us in Ephesians 6: 11:

'put on the whole armor of God so that we can be able to stand against the Devil's schemes.'

What is needed is not something that comes from us but that which comes from God. The armor of God is given because ours does not work effectively. Ours is a paper fence in a flood. Our armor is made by us, and we have put in on the wrong way, we have it upside down and even when it fits, it is not suitable for the attacks that we will face in life. The tragedy is that Christians who place their faith in the church are ill-equipped for battle. The Mass will not save you from the schemes of the Devil, nor will your infant baptism, or your adult baptism, nor will your rituals or your sermons. It is only God who can save you and it is only God who can protect you.

Christian Fascists might dare to go further and try to adopt the language of Paul to construct some principles we can live by. When speaking of the armor of God in the New Testament Paul uses some keywords such as faith, hope and love (1 Thessalonians 5: 7-9). In Ephesians he speaks of truth, righteousness, peace, faith, and the Spirit (Ephesians 6: 11-18). The fascists will ignore the metaphor of the armor as silly fiction but will give beautiful sermons on love, faith, and hope, and mix it in with the importance of trying our best to love others, especially our own, and build our kingdoms on earth and return our nation to our Christian roots.

The Bible does not offer principles to live by or ethics to obey but presents us with a Savior who has gone before us and stood in our place so we would not need to stand against Diabolos alone. This the Christian Fascist will avoid talking about because they can talk about love, but they will do their best to ignore the embodiment of love, Jesus Christ. They are offended by him as he gets in the way of their kingdom on earth, the Christian nation. But the bible proclaims that Jesus by his life lived for God, and by his death on the cross for all who believe he stood against evil and overcame it. He put on the full armor of God against the Devil so we would not stand alone.

Indeed, it was Christ who road-tested the armor of God. In Ephesians, Paul mentions truth, righteousness, and peace as three pieces of this armor of God. Jesus put on all three. Jesus lived by the truth, and he embodied the truth for by his arrival, life, and death, he told the world who God is, how he might be known, and what needed to be done so people might know him. Jesus repeatedly told his disciples:

'that the Son of Man must be betrayed into the hands of sinful men and be crucified, and that he would rise again on the third day,' (Luke 24:7).

He did not lie but was honest to all. He often used the phrase *'I tell you the truth,'* (for example in In Matthew 11: 11). Indeed, there was truthfulness in his words and in his life (see John 8). Jesus even said that he embodied the truth when he said that he was the way the truth and the life and that no one came to the Father, except through him (John 14: 6). Before Pilate, Jesus identified with the truth. John records in 18: 37:

"You are a king, then!" said Pilate. Jesus answered, "you say that I am a king. In fact, the reason I was born and came into the world is to testify to the truth. Everyone on the side of truth listens to me.'

Are Christian Fascists prepared to say that *'everyone on the side of truth listens to Christ?'* It is a bold statement for Jesus to make. Can they take refuge in Christ alone? I don't think so. Jesus is an obstacle to their Culture War and their fascist desires for national Christianity. To follow the truth, they must leave these at the door to the kingdom of God as no such nonsense is welcome there. Maybe they should check with their political masters first.

Jesus also put on the armor of God by arming himself with righteousness. Christ lived a sinless life proclaiming the Bible so that he fulfilled the Law of Moses and lived a life that no one else was able to do. He fulfilled all righteousness, and when he died on the cross, he died as one righteous before God, not as a sinner, not as one guilty under the law, but he became sin for us so that we might receive the righteousness of God. Paul writes in Romans 10: 4:

'Christ is the culmination of the law so that there may be righteousness for everyone who believes.'

Paul even says in Galatians 4: 3-5:

'So also, when we were underage, we were in slavery under the elemental spiritual forces of the world. But when the set time had fully come, God sent his Son, born of a woman, born under the law, to redeem those under the law, that we might receive adoption to sonship.'

This righteousness is not from us, or from the Christian or the Christian Fascist, but from God. Paul explains this in 2 Corinthians 5: 21:

'God made him who had no sin to be sin for us, so that in him we might become the righteousness of God.'

The righteousness has nothing to do with us, it is not our good works or living a good life or living according to the standard of the church. Nor is it Christian Fascism, being a good white supremacist. It is simply to receive by faith what Christ has done. Indeed, that is why we call Jesus, the Saviour because he saves.

Jesus also puts on the armor of peace, both in terms of his identity and the fruit of his life. This might seem a contradiction in terms of wearing armor, but it is a confirmation of the identity of Jesus and for all who seek to follow him. Luke 2: 14 reads that the angels said at his birth:

'Glory to God in the highest heaven, and on earth peace to those on whom his favor rests.'

When he saw his disciples after his resurrection his first words to them were *'peace be with you'* (Luke 24: 36; John 20: 19). Jesus spoke to reassure his disciples and give them comfort and words of peace. He said in John 14: 27:

'Peace I leave with you; my peace I give you. I do not give to you as the world gives. Do not let your hearts be troubled and do not be afraid.'

Not only was his arrival one of peace and his life and his words, but his death and resurrection brought about peace with God. Paul writes in Romans 5: 1-3:

'Therefore, since we have been justified through faith, we have peace with God through our Lord Jesus Christ, through whom we have gained access by faith into this grace in which we now stand. And we boast in the hope of the glory of God.'

Freedom from instability

One of the sports we used to play as children but that you don't see much these days was the *'tug of war.'* In this contest, two teams needed to pull on a rope that had a knot in the middle and a bandana tied around it. There were marks on the ground which showed where each team had to avoid being pulled across. It was backbreaking, but it was fun. I don't see it these days, perhaps because it was rather unpredictable and there was always the possibility of someone being hurt. In the age of *'helicopter parenting,'* it is probably a casualty of that way of thinking.

Success in the tug of war depended almost entirely on who was holding the end of the rope. The bigger and stronger that person, the more stable the rope would be and the less instability the rope-pullers would feel. The big strong boys or girls would wrap the rope around them and dig their heels into the dirt for the showdown. God's armor prevents instability in the defense of the Christian against the Devil. He says in Ephesians 6: 11,

'put on the whole armor of God so that you will be able to stand against the Devil's schemes.'

The goal of putting on the armor of God is to be able to stand. Like the anchor of the tug of war, the aim is to stand your ground and the armor is designed to be able to do just that. What is interesting about Paul's image might be lost to the reader, especially to the Christian or person familiar with the text. There is something missing in this verse, and in verse 13 which is similar:

'take up all of the armor of God that you may be able to resist in the evil day, and having worked out all things, to stand.'

You might have noticed it. The position of the Christian wearing the armor of God is not for attack but for defense. There is no mention of attack, save for deflection, there is no mention of moving forward save for standing one's ground, there is no mention of fighting save for quenching the darts of Diabolos (Ephesians 6: 16).

The struggle of the Christian is stand one's ground, it is to fight, but it is not to attack. This would have been a strange metaphor for Paul's readers, and it is a strange one to listen to today as America, England, Australia, France, and Germany, among others, have all declared war on Russia, and soon, China. The Europeans started two world wars and before that bathed the continent in blood for centuries and now, they want more of it, that is the so-called *'Christian nations,'* so eager to go to war as ever.

Even the heartland of European fascism, Germany, is openly touting nuclear war with Russia, and rearming for a third tilt at world power. America will risk nuclear war and the devastation that will bring to prevent any nation from wanting to share the bounty of the earth with them. Surely there is enough to go around and for all to share, but America wants it all for itself and the West wants to rule the world and have all nations bow to them like the empires of ancient times. They are not in charge of course. This insanity could only be devised by Diabolos, who is the god of this world, the one they say, *'in whom they trust.'* It is certainly not Jesus Christ. Linking America or any nation with God's plan for humanity is unforgivable blasphemy.

We cannot look to the insanity of the West for aid in understanding Paul's image of a defensive attack. But we can look to martial arts especially in the East, as many of them would understand exactly what Paul is saying and what he is talking about. The principle is simple: if you can defend your position, and hold your ground, you can hold your position indefinitely, you cannot be dislodged. The key then is the nature of defense. So, what does Paul mean by standing your ground against the Devil's schemes?

First, Paul says that if you put on the armor of God, you are able, or have the power to make your stand. The standing depends on the putting on of the armor of God. If you do not have the armor of God, then you will not be able to stand. Second, attack is not required in God's army. The goal is to stand your ground, hold your position and deflect attack. This is in keeping with Christianity as being fundamentally about peace, not war. The question for many of us must be *'why not attack?'* and *'why not destroy?'*

I think the answer lies in the fact that we live in a world shaped by cosmic and spiritual realities, at the center of which is the cross, the place where the Son of God died. What was achieved at the cross was decisive, it was comprehensive, and it shaped the cosmos. All of creation is still living with the echo of that day. All Christians live under the shadow of the cross and receive the benefits that flow from the death of the Son of God.

What is being contested in this world is that event, the person who is at the center of that event, and the consequences of that event for all people and all of creation. There is not a new war to be fought, nor a new enemy to be sought out, but it is simply the continuation of the conflict that began at creation, reached its culmination at the cross and the empty tomb and echoes across creation until today. Part of the answer is also that the battle comes to us. James says:

'resist the Devil and he will flee from you' (James 4:7).

Peter says much the same thing in 1 Peter 5: 8-10:

'Be alert and of sober mind. Your enemy the devil prowls around like a roaring lion looking for someone to devour. Resist him, standing firm in the faith, because you know that the family of believers throughout the world is undergoing the same kind of sufferings. And the God of all grace, who called you to his eternal glory in Christ, after you have suffered a little while, will himself restore you and make you strong, firm, and steadfast.'

Peter and James emphasize the resistance of Diabolos while Paul places emphasis here on an active defense using God's armor. Peter expects his readers also to *'stand'* by *'standing firm,'* by being encouraged by the witness of others and the power of God to enable them to stand against him. This is about stability and God's armor provides this.

The battle comes to Christians because they are the representatives of God's kingdom on earth. Our citizenship is in heaven (Philippians 3: 20), we are just pilgrims and strangers in this land, passing through (1 Peter 2: 10-12) and we are the followers of Jesus. This means that we face persecution and attack. Jesus makes this clear in the Gospels (Mark 10:30, Matthew 5: 11, Matthew 24: 9, Luke 21: 12). For example, Jesus says in John's Gospel 15: 20:

'Remember what I told you: 'A servant is not greater than his master.'
If they persecuted me, they will persecute you also.'

The reason for the defensive, not offensive position will become clearer later, and it really goes to the heart of the problem of Christian Fascism which is the greatest threat to Christianity in the West today. This spiritual battle is not primarily a battle within us, as it is a battle against us, as Diabolos seeks to take out the people who witness the goodness of God found in the Lord Jesus Christ. Christians are not to make their stand against the nation, the state, the culture, or people in society, but against the Devil's schemes, and that is the reason for them to put on the full armor of God.

Now, this might all be new to you. Certainly, in many Christian circles, the enemy is someone else, some other group, often a political or sectarian group, but notice that Paul makes no mention of them. He doesn't even mention his own people as being worthy of attention. Christian Fascists, for example, claim to be Christians but they rarely talk about Jesus unless it is to enlist him in their latest crusade.

Paul cuts to the chase and so do we. Paul goes to the heart of it because he wants Christians to stand, and not fall, and so do we. Paul places the hope of the Christian not in the state or the church or doctrine or sect, but simply in Christ and so do we. This book is to equip you to stand without fear because we stand with the one who brings true freedom, Jesus. The armor of God is to enable us to defend our position against the schemes of the Devil, not to attack other people.

Freedom from methodology

We live in an age of planning. It used to be that the old Soviet Union and Chinese Communists were addicted to planning. They employed famous *'five-year plans,'* especially the Chinese. I am not sure why it was five years. Perhaps it is a good term, but it could easily have been four or three, or six. The Soviet Union and others used to be called a *'planned economy,'* and that is what it was. Everything was organized and controlled and planned, in contrast to the chaotic craziness of capitalism.

We don't hear the term *'planned economy'* much these days except in demographic policies such as the term *'planned parenthood'* and so on. Planning has instead come full circle and now we are all active planners – we have diaries and planners, and schedules and meetings, and these are organized down to the latest minute. Our entire lives are planned and scheduled.

There is nothing wrong with planning and schedules but like all things that may have usefulness, we can end up being trapped by them. They can become a terrible burden and we can suffer under an unreasonable set of unfinished tasks, and they can rise like an ogre and overwhelm us. Our lives can be defined by what we have failed to do rather than what we have done, and this instils a sense of guilt and shame. Paul tells us in Ephesians 1: 11 to:

put on the whole armor of God so that we may be able to make a stand against the Devil's schemes.'

Before we address the text itself, we need to find some comfort in the words of Jesus to act as a balm or antidote for those stuck in the grip of excessive planning. Jesus said in Matthew 6: 25-34:

'Therefore, I tell you, do not be anxious about your life, what you will eat or what you will drink, nor about your body, what you will put on. Is not life more than food, and the body more than clothing? Look at the birds of the air: they neither sow nor reap nor gather into barns, and yet your heavenly Father feeds them. Are you not of more value than they? And which of you by being anxious can add a single hour to his span of life?

And why are you anxious about clothing? Consider the lilies of the field, how they grow: they neither toil nor spin, yet I tell you, even Solomon in all his glory was not arrayed like one of these. But if God so clothes the grass of the field, which today is alive and tomorrow is thrown into the oven, will he not much more clothe you, O you of little faith? Therefore, do not be anxious, saying, 'What shall we eat?' or 'What shall we drink?' or 'What shall we wear?' For the Gentiles seek after all these things, and your heavenly Father knows that you need them all. But seek first the kingdom of God and his righteousness, and all these things will be added to you. Therefore, do not be anxious about tomorrow, for tomorrow will be anxious for itself. Sufficient for the day is its own trouble.'

It is interesting to know that Jesus never uses the word *'method'* nor does Paul, nor does James or John or Peter, to describe the Christian life. The word method, where we get our word *'methodology,'* comes from the Greek word methodeia which means methods or schemes. There are only two places in the whole New Testament they are used, and they are both used in a negative way. They are both in Ephesians and they both refer to the activities of those who wish evil. First, Ephesians 4: 14:

'Then we will no longer be infants, tossed back and forth by the waves, and blown here and there by every wind of teaching and by the cunning and craftiness of people in their deceitful scheming.'

In the Greek it refers to the *'scheming of deceit'* when using the word *'method.'* The cunning and craftiness of men are contrasted with speaking the truth in love of God's people. The friends of Diabolos plan and scheme, while God's people speak the truth in love in the power of the Spirit. There are plenty of examples of such scheming in the Bible. The Bible is very clear on how evil works and expresses itself. The wicked are often known by the actions they plan, they scheme, and they wait to pounce. This method is perhaps the Greek version of *'laying in wait'* or waiting to attack. We should not be surprised at the wickedness in the world. For example, in Proverbs 1: 10-12:

'My son, if sinners entice you, do not yield to them. If they say, "Come along, let us lie in wait for blood, let us ambush the innocent without cause, let us swallow them alive like Sheol, and whole like those descending into the Pit.'

This is the kind of scheming Paul has in mind. It is premeditated, it is planned, it has a method to it.

The second reference to a method in the New Testament has to do with Ephesians 6: 11 where Christians are to stand against the schemes or the methods of the Devil. There is a scheme to his thinking, a craft a method. Today we would say a guidebook, an instruction manual to tricking up Christians and bringing them down to ruin, to slander the Son of God. Satan has a method, a plan, a scheme, and the Bible always sees them in a negative light. These methods are not positive, and they are designed to destroy the witness and testimony of Christians.

The whole aim of the armor of God is to take a stand against the Devil and his schemes. There are perhaps several reasons why the church refuses to tell the truth about the Devil. The first I have mentioned before. There is so much money in it. There are billions to be made in scaring people out of their wits thinking that the Devil is lurking around every corner or on their lips or in their hearts. American Christian Fascists are the Gold Standard when it comes to lying about Satan.

The second reason is perhaps that many do not believe there is a spirit with the name Diabolos, and he has no place in the cosmic order. It is my experience that most ritualistic or traditional priests have no real faith in God, it is simply a career choice for them, as they wait out for retirement, so if they do not believe in God, they are unlikely to believe in the Devil.

I have mentioned the third reason, in reference to evangelicals who think that somehow the death of Jesus also killed off Satan which is puzzling because all the New Testament writers affirm his power, intent, existence, and character. There is even the bizarre reference in Jude to the Devil, urging Christians not to slander even him (Jude 8-9):

'*Yet in the same way these dreamers defile their bodies, reject authority, and slander glorious beings. But even the archangel Michael, when he disputed with the devil over the body of Moses, did not presume to bring a slanderous charge against him, but said, "The Lord rebuke you!"*'

The final reason why the Devil is a problem for the church is that like Jesus, he is getting in the way of Christian Fascism and their war against people. Paul clearly states that the point of the armor of God is to make a stand against the Devil's schemes. It is not designed to make a stand against people, even wicked people. This is the opposite message of the fake gospel of Christian Fascism which is now the terminal cancer eating the church today, devouring it. Some Christian Fascists will enlist the fear of the Devil to whip up support for the political agenda, but it is usually guilt by association. Some opposite groups or group of people are Satanic for whatever reason as they stand in the way of rebuilding a nation for God.

For most, however, the Devil gets in the way because they want to rebuild their Christian nation, with Christian values, Christian laws, and Christian people. The clever ones have realized that once they start talking about something supernatural, then the entire edifice falls, and people see through the cracks of their sterile, dead, godless kingdom of man and see instead the hope and glory of the kingdom of God.

To achieve their *'slaughterhouse in waiting,'* which is the synonym for a Christian nation, they need to slander the Devil as much as they slander God and pretend neither exist so as they do not challenge the hell they wish to create on earth. Just look at the Great War and the second Great War, organized by nations that all claimed to be Christian, certainly in the European theatre. This of course is music to the ears of Diabolos, and he is the chief architect of Christian Fascism for every Christian nation that uses his methods ends up closing their Bibles, slandering God, and destroying the reputation of Christians around the world. Just look at America and its lust for war, amid the blasphemous chorus of *'God bless America.'*

4   OUR STRUGGLE

Our Struggle

One of the vilest, most awful texts ever composed by a man was, for over a decade, the most popular, most-loved book in pre-war Germany. From its initial publication in 1925, it quickly became the book that couples would be given at their marriage ceremonies, everyone knew of it, most had read it, and it was undoubtedly one of the key devices for the effective rise of the Nazi Party.

The idea that Germans did not know what Hitler had planned for the Jews is a lie. I still hear it today from fascists. They knew. Hitler told them. It was in his book, titled *'My Struggle.'* In this scribal obscenity, Hitler lays out his ideology and plans for exterminating Jews very carefully and cleverly. In fact, his rise to power surfed on the wave of unrelenting Anti-Semitism in Germany, facilitated in part by the Lutheran national church, which was deeply anti-Jewish and had been since it was founded. Martin Luther indeed had said many wonderful things about faith in Christ when he was not hating Jews.

I encountered *'My Struggle,'* while researching my book on the rise of fascism, which is currently being prepared for publication. I didn't want to read it, but I needed to find a few quotes. I was comforted by the fact that my edition of the book had a preface written by a Jewish journalist who had fled Hitler in the 1930s and I reasoned that if this Holocaust survivor had opened its pages, then I could as well. I knew that by opening this book, I would be stepping into filth, for that is what fascism in all its forms is – pure filth. Fascism is the great evil of human creation. There can be no compromise with it.

The book's preface was a sufficient framework to use to navigate the bile, hatred, and frenzied vitriol against Jews and I trod carefully, knowing that I was reading a book that helped to cause the murder of over six million Jews along with homosexuals, masons, gypsies, and opponents of the Third Reich. I trod cautiously as I did not want to unsettle the dead, who were led like lambs to the slaughter, and whose bones were burned, scattered, and tossed like garbage. As a Christian and follower of Jesus, and deeply aware of the church's appalling relationship with Judaism over the centuries, I walked with deep respect, in silence, for the unforgotten dead.

What I found astonished me. I was speechless. Three things struck me. First, I could find no quote for my book that satisfied me, for Hitler did not stay on one subject long enough for me to find one. How his book was popular amongst the German ruling class of the 1930s was astounding. It was not that Hitler invented Anti-Semitism, it was already there, it was knee-deep, it was ingrained in German culture. As a piece of literature, it was almost impossible to read, and I could not read beyond a few paragraphs here and there before giving up.

The second thing that struck me was that Hitler was not mad, but a very clever, manipulative, and cunning person, for what he did was strip a human being of all their rich complexity, their variety, and nuances, and influences, to create a person in his image so he could murder them. That person was his definition of a *'Jew.'* This was classic European Anti-Semitism.

Alfred Marshall, the father of neoclassical economics did the same with the discipline of economics in the nineteenth century. Economics before Marshall included history, culture, and politics, even class (Adam Smith and David Ricardo accepted the notion of *'class'*), but Marshall disposed of all of them in favor of economic science. He stripped humanity of richness, culture, subtlety, and value to create the *'economic man,'* what economists call the *'individual.'* Some call Marshall's economic genius *'methodological individualism.'* Marshall created the individual to pretend that economics was a science, which it isn't, but his intentions were not nefarious.

Hitler's goal, however, was to create a definition of a Jewish person so that their removal from society would not be noticed, or lamented, for everything they were, everything they believed in, and everything they said opposed German culture. They were, in Hitler's definition, against Germany, they undermined German values and what it meant to be German. That was his goal. It was largely achieved in 6 years when he took over and few Germans opposed the persecution and then extermination of Jews.

Even today, the grandchildren of fascists lie to my face and say that only a tiny group of SS officers knew what was going on. Tragically, and astoundingly, I have been hearing it more and more, and that is the argument from people seeking to defend Hitler and the Nazis in their so-called *'struggle'* against Jews.

The third thing that struck me when I opened Mein Kampf was that Hitler sounded very familiar. I had heard him before. In fact, I had heard him a lot growing up in Australia. He is on the radio every morning, with the radio personalities who have the people they hate, the people they blame for the problems in society. Hitler is in parliament and on the voices of politicians who tell me that we have too many foreigners or too many refugees.

Most disturbingly of all, he is in the pulpit of many of our churches. Yes, Hitler is there too. In fact, he is experiencing a revival in the West in thousands of pulpits in across many nations. Some people, mainly academics don't know what it is, and so they call it the wrong thing. They call it Christian nationalism, but they are wrong. There is nothing wrong with flag-waving or loving your nation. We should call this religious cancer its proper name in honor of its true father, its true allegiance, and its true origin. It is Christian Fasism, or Fascism in the name of Christianity.

Maybe you are a Christian Fascist. Certainly, if you go to church in America or Australia or Canada or New Zealand or Great Britain, chances are you might be, or you may have come under the influence of a Christian Fascist, or read their books, listened to their sermons, read their online posts. I would guess that most church-going people in the West today are either Christian Fascists or people with deep sympathies for the beliefs, ideals, and values of Christian Fascism.

When Christians give up on Christ, they become fascists, every time. It is not surprising, since fascism comes from national Christianity. It didn't just appear in the 1920s out of the blue. Sadly, many simply cannot tell the difference between Christianity and Fascism anymore; the lines have been so blurred. If you are not a Christian, the response to fascism might be war, the process of steady destruction through aerial bombardment and missiles. It worked last time, and seems to be working in Ukraine, but at a terrible cost. No one truly wins in war, and it is not the war Christians ought to be involved. Ours is a spiritual war, not a physical war.

The Western Church is truly fascist for they are denouncing Russian intervention in Ukraine but will fall silent when the war is over and will say nothing. They don't believe in a spiritual war unless the government tells them to promote it, and they will keep their Bible closed until they are told by the state to open it.

I am a Christian and war is a sin, all wars, and that includes the War on Terror and the Twenty Years War in the Middle East. It is fascinating to hear Christians say that they don't want any assets tied up with Russia because war is evil, but they have assets tied up in America, and there is no greater warmongering nation than America. This is Christian Fascism at work. They don't know the difference anymore. They are such dreadful hypocrites.

So, to Christian Fascists I say this, you will not listen to me, but you will have to listen to God and his word the Bible. Fascism is a sin and I hope that you will see it and recoil in horror, turn back to God and follow Jesus. If in the process, your entire world falls so be it, because what does it profit a person if they gain the whole world and yet lose their soul? There is no place in the kingdom of God for fascists, they wouldn't want to be there anyway.

Hitler was wrong. Fascism is always wrong. The Bible says little about liberalism and a little about socialism – we are free to choose the politics – but fascism is always, everywhere condemned. It has many names and takes many forms, but it has one father. His name is Diabolos. Remember him, fascists? His watermark is on lots of sermons now, his fingerprints in many pulpits, and his language in many churches.

All I can do, as a Christian is to remind you of the Bible, and for those of you who are not Christians or have been hurt by Christian fascists, know this: you are not alone, and not all Christians stand with the church, and not all Christians stand with fascists. Many Christians simply follow Jesus, or that is their goal each day as their life is a relationship with God, not a ritual, theirs is a faith, not a religion, and for them, God is big, he is real, and he can be known by anyone, and he has no favorites.

I am sure that many of you have never heard these words from Paul the apostle. Certainly, the church will try to hide it from you, as these words oppose everything they say, and they need to say it because fascism brings in the money and they can live the good life while they keep the Bible closed and you ignorant. It comes from Ephesians 6: 12:

'For our struggle is not against flesh and blood, but against the rulers, against the authorities, against the powers of this dark world and against the spiritual forces of evil in the heavenly realms.'

Our focus for the moment is the first part:

'our struggle is not against flesh and blood.'

For the Christian, what a relief, for the fascist, this is the horror of horrors and the blackest darkness.

Freedom from standing alone

It was a cold and bitter night in Kyoto. It was the middle of winter. Lectures had finished for the day, and I had an evening meal at a local pub that served barbequed chicken on skewers. The place was always full of people, squashed together on the wooden counters, polished by years of customers rising and sitting. A huge mask of the mountain goblin hung over the entrance, his vacant eyes surveying the room, dense with cigarette smoke. The chefs stood in the middle of the room running back and forth, cooking, simmering, grilling, and shouting calls to welcome and farewell customers.

After a while, I left, catching a bus from there to the old Imperial Palace, shrouded in darkness, except for the watchful eye of the local police officers. I made my way up a darkened staircase to an old room, lit up, to a table and chairs set up. Bill was already there. He had the Bible notes prepared, copied from his study bible and we sat shivering while the kerosene heater worked itself on.

There, every Thursday we studied the bible together. Bill was an academic and a man of faith. Only true faith would compel a man to travel on such bitterly cold nights to study the Bible with what was only one or two people each week. For me, gathering with others who called Jesus their Lord, was one of the greatest blessings one could ask for during those years in Japan. We were few, so few, but our conversations were deep, and our fellowship strong.

Christians need to gather with others and Christ was always present, he always is when his children gather even in two and three in the deepest winter. Paul was reminded of this when he sought Christian fellowship with others in Corinth. He experienced intense persecution from his fellow Jews for even talking about Jesus and he fell into despondency. Jesus appeared to him in a vision and told him. Acts 18: 9-10:

'Do not be afraid; keep on speaking, do not be silent. For I am with you, and no one is going to attack and harm you, because I have many people in this city.'

Paul stayed and he found others who followed Jesus. There are many of God's people everywhere and if you seek them, you will find them. I did not say go to church, for most who go there are not God's people, not anymore. I am talking about having faith that God will bring people into your life to encourage you and that you might encourage them. The church is often the default option for lazy Christians who gave up trusting God long ago. You are blessed if you meet a fellow Christian on the road or at work or in your family, or through other serendipitous ways.

Christians are also known by their common struggle. Paul writes in Ephesians 6: 12 of *'our struggle,'* and it is a common struggle. We do not stand alone as followers of Jesus. He writes:

'For our struggle is not against flesh and blood, but against the rulers, against the authorities, against the powers of this dark world, and against the spiritual forces of evil in the heavenly realms.'

This struggle, for all Christians, is a common one, it involves all, and none are excluded. Early Christians seemed to have a much greater comradery than exists today. Churchgoers only join forces against a common public enemy as they usually cannot abide each other.

It was not so in the beginning. Christians were simply those who had faith in the risen Lord Jesus Christ, and this included everyone, of every background, creed, culture, language, or social standing. Paul writes to the Romans *'your faith is being reported all over the world'* (Romans 1: 8). To the Ephesians he wrote in 1: 15 *'I heard about your faith in the Lord Jesus and your love for all God's people.'* In Colossians 1: 4 he wrote: *'we have heard of your faith in Christ Jesus and of the love you have for all God's people.'*

In their common struggle, Christians knew they did not struggle alone, because their faith was genuine, it was real. There is only one verse comparable in the New Testament to the word *'struggle'* in Ephesians 6: 12, and it is in Romans 15: 30. It is sometimes translated as struggle, but this is not strictly correct. In Greek, the word is *'sunagónizomai,'* and you will see another English word tucked away in there: agony. It means to agonize with or strive together. In the ESV it reads *'I appeal to you, brothers, by our Lord Jesus Christ and by the love of the Spirit, to strive together with me in your prayers to God on my behalf'* (Romans 15: 30). Christians do not stand alone. Ours is a common struggle and we strive together in the name of the Lord Jesus, in the power of the Spirit.

Freedom from wrestling alone

One of the most remarkable sports is sumo, from Japan. Two incredibly large men wrestle on a small mat surrounded by thousands of fans, an event deeply ritualized and adored by millions. The contests last only a few moments, and those seated too close to the mat can be surprised by being squashed by one of the wrestlers, but it is all part of the incredible experience.

Sumo is one of the many forms of ancient wrestling around the world. In the Hebrew Bible, wrestling is mentioned in the book of Genesis in that enigmatic encounter involving the second and duplicitous son of Isaac, Jacob and whom the text calls a man (32: 24), implying it was God (32: 28-30). Jacob does not wrestle with an angel. Through this wrestling match, he is given a new name – Israel, and he becomes a new man, blessed by God.

This is how we tend to picture the Christian life in all its complexity, as a personal, individual wrestling match that we do independently of others, without the aid of others, without their prayers and support, a little bit like John the Baptist in the wilderness with his locusts and wild honey or one of the prophets of old.

Our Western Christianity has been so unbelievably corrupted by the pagan individualism of liberalism, and the incoherent mumbo jumbo of *'class struggle,'* that listening to God's Word is like trying to wade through a swamp blindfolded surrounded by rabid gnats singing *'the star-spangled banner in Russian.'* Christian Fascists or Fascists who call themselves Christians, cannot tell the difference between the philosophy of the founding Fathers of the American Constitution and the Bible. The Bible confers no *'God-given rights'* to anyone outside of Christ, nor are these individually conferred, nor are they bound to a nation geographically defined. We are trying to unpack and unravel the verse of Paul in his letter to the Ephesians chapter 6 and verse 12:

'For we do not wrestle against flesh and blood, but against the rulers, against the authorities, against the cosmic powers over this present darkness, against the spiritual forces of evil in the heavenly places.'

This struggle is not an individualistic one, but a communal one, one enjoyed by all who follow Jesus, both living and dead, it is *'our struggle,'* or *'our wrestling.'* This is because while faith is someone everyone must decide for themselves, one is never alone in the kingdom of God. God's kingdom is for God's people and those who are his are among his people, both in this world and the next.

We do not wrestle alone. What a blessing it is to hear that someone will pray for you. What sadness it is if someone claims to be a Christian and does not pray with you. Becoming a Christian is not a journey into loneliness or the long path to a hermitage or monastery – they are for priests who wish to escape from their duties. Becoming a Christian means finding a new family in Christ, a new identity, and a new beginning. Some words of comfort for those who think we wrestle alone.

We are members of a new nation not under God but with God. Peter wrote in 1 Peter 2: 9-10:

'But you are a chosen race, a royal priesthood, a holy nation, a people for his own possession, that you may proclaim the excellencies of him who called you out of darkness into his marvelous light. Once you were not a people, but now you are God's people; once you had not received mercy, but now you have received mercy.'

We are as close to God as we can be by virtue of Christ. Paul wrote in Ephesians 2: 12-13:

'remember that you were at that time separated from Christ, alienated from the commonwealth of Israel and strangers to the covenants of promise, having no hope and without God in the world. But now in Christ Jesus you who once were far off have been brought near by the blood of Christ.'

We are equal, full members of God's family. Paul writes in Galatians 4: 3-7:

'In the same way we also, when we were children, were enslaved to the elementary principles of the world. But when the fullness of time had come, God sent forth his Son, born of woman, born under the law, to redeem those who were under the law, so that we might receive adoption as sons. And because you are sons, God has sent the Spirit of his Son into our hearts, crying, "Abba! Father!" So, you are no longer a slave, but a son, and if a son, then an heir through God.'

Being a Christian means, we never wrestle alone.

Freedom from stupidity

We have been exploring together the phrase 'our struggle is not against flesh and blood,' taken from Paul's letter to the Ephesians chapter 6, verse 12 where he says:

'For we do not wrestle against flesh and blood, but against the rulers, against the authorities, against the cosmic powers over this present

darkness, against the spiritual forces of evil in the heavenly places.' (ESV).

This verse demolishes Christian Fascism in one blow because Paul tells the Ephesians, and he tells us that *'we do not wrestle against flesh and blood.'* Fascism teaches that the problems in life are due always to people, or groups of people who are the enemies of the nation, those who are undermining it, bringing it into disrepute or corruption, and who need to be stopped. Only fascists thinks like this.

The church is full of fascists who think like this. Their list of suspects is long, but it is the usual suspects: people of different religions, women, foreigners, homosexuals and other gendered minorities, Jews, the poor, the left or the right, and other Christians. For fascists, the problems facing society are always caused by people, and the solution is to return to the past, to the good old days, or some reimagined version of it. To get there, the church wants the sword so they can start punishing people or killing them if they can.

There may even be a glimmer of support for Christian Fascism in the Bible if it were not for one, single verb in this verse of Paul's to the Ephesians. It is not hidden. This verb is in plain sight, and it is a remarkable verb for upon it hinges the entire Christian faith. Worlds turn upon this verb. I prefer the reading of the Greek as follows: *'For us wrestling is not against flesh and blood.'* It is simply a matter of form. The ESV *'we do not wrestle against flesh and blood,'* and that is fine too, but the Greek verb is 'estin.' It comes from the Greek *'I am,'* or *'I exist.'* It is the *'first person singular present indicative.'* What this means it is not in the past tense. Paul is not saying *'was not,'* or implying anything of the sort. For Christians, *'our struggle is not,'* is what he is clearly saying. He is not saying *'our struggle was not.'*

There are two immediate implications from this remarkable verb. First, for Fascists. Paul says that *'we do not wrestle against flesh and blood.'* Our wrestling, combative as it is, is not against people, and this renders Christian Fascism null and void. Our fight is not with any group in our society, and we do not wrestle against them. They are not our enemy.

In fact, a follower of Jesus has no real enemy among humanity as Jesus taught us to love our enemies. How quickly the fascists fell silent on quoting Jesus. During Covid Hysteria, the fascists were yelling for us to *'love our neighbor and get vaccinated,'* but how many of these Christian Fascists are telling us to *'love our enemy,'* which is apparently Russia, and *'do good to them'*? Few, if any, certainly not in America, a land drowning in Russophobia.

Nor I am not talking about *'hate the sin and love the sinner,'* or that equally superficial nonsense of *'what would Jesus do?'* Jesus did not own a gun, nor would he support the right to bear arms, or defend your *'God-given rights.'* Are they asking for the invocation of the blessing of the Lord Jesus Christ or is it the god of this world? It is never clear. Maybe if you don't know the identity of the God you are invoking, it is best to leave him out of it.

The second implication is that many evangelicals are plain wrong about our contest with Diabolos. The reason for their *'error'* or *'omission,'* is that they have a faulty view of the atonement, which is the death of Christ, as well as a faulty understanding of Paul who wrote Ephesians as Romans.

These days, many men and women who once talked about Jesus are now talking about morality, social justice, and citizenship, which is all fine and good, but don't pretend it is for one minute Christianity. As millions leave the church in droves in the West, the churches are changing their message away from the plain gospel of God's grace to whatever can keep their church doors open.

The old nationalist churches are disappearing into cultural Christianity and eventual oblivion. The traditionalists in Roman and English churches don't care since they didn't believe in God anyway, but their churches are expensive to run, and they all want to keep the good stipends. They will solicit funds from the state, with strings attached. The new Christian Fascists in the ruling class with their morality crusades, seek to draw support from the middle class, exploiting all their fears of the present and future into a bundle they can easily translate into people who can be blamed. But if so many churches and Christians are fighting the wrong war, what does Paul mean that we *'do not wrestle against flesh and blood?'*

Freedom from futility

As societies become more complex, political, and economic answers often become more intractable, especially when material interests are involved, obscuring educational institutions and media. In other words, when you run a village, life is simple, but it still has its own challenges.

Running a city or a nation involves vast organizational and logistical engineering, cooperation, collusion, mechanisms, and so on. Imagine running America, China, Russia, or India. Many of the problems facing people are technological, administrative, logistical, and so on. We could argue about the underlying structures and material interests and power relations till we are blue in the face, but the simple fact is that it is miracle a modern society works at all, even remotely as well as they do.

I assumed, quite naively that as societies evolved to more complex forms of organization, people would naturally adapt towards an acceptance of the dynamics in these processes simply as part of their daily routine, that these *'facts of life'* would act as a counterbalance against prejudice, stupidity, futility, and idiocy that plagued earlier, simpler societies. I naturally assumed that with the invention of the microchip and semiconductor, the cell phone, and the net, people would realize the rich tapestry of human interaction, that crime would decline, and that with education people would overcome prejudice.

How wrong I was. People are just as prejudiced today as ever, crime is rampant, and even educated people live only a diet of fake news, gossip, and propaganda. The more complex society becomes the easier it is to persecute people and especially to locate, harass and eliminate those groups allegedly responsible for all the problems in our complex society. This is the paradox of post-modern life. The more technological we become, the more prone we are to see monsters and want to destroy them.

That is why Paul's letter to the Ephesians is so relevant today. It speaks to us 2,000 years after it was composed. It carries the weight of Holy Scripture, in other words, the Bible, which your local church of eager fascists pretends to believe in, but they don't like Paul because he was not a fascist. Fascists blame innocent people for problems they didn't cause.

Fascists are driven by the lynch mentality, the logic of mobs. They are the opposite of Paul. If he blamed anyone in life, he blamed himself for his failings of youth, his desires for revenge and killing, and his religious fanaticism. He certainly advised people to avoid trouble and danger, but Paul loved people, and in Ephesians 6: 12 he tells his readers quite remarkable given that he had so many enemies that *'we do not wrestle against flesh and blood.'* The church today should take notice and fascists should cease their morality crusades because you are fighting against God. What does Paul mean by flesh and blood? There is evidence within his other writings that give us a clue to the meaning of the phrase *'flesh and blood.'*

In his first letter to the Corinthians chapter 15 and verse 50, Paul is speaking of life and death, of the end of the human body and its journey and the arrival of the heavenly body and the world beyond. This verse reads:

'I tell you this, brothers: flesh and blood cannot inherit the kingdom of God, nor does the perishable inherit the imperishable.'

On one level, it poses more questions than it answers, but Paul seems to be saying here that people as people, as bones, flesh, and earthly stuff, cannot inherit the kingdom of God which is spiritual in nature. The important thing for us here is that the phrase is the same. Paul says, *'flesh and blood,'* and in all translations, this phrase is retained as far as I know. Most are reluctant to change the original in Greek, which I find interesting.

Put simply, Paul is saying, we are not wrestling against people, we are not struggling against people, and we are not fighting against people. Thus, in this one verse, Paul kills Marxism, Liberalism, and Fascism dead. Liberals say individuals compete against one another, Marx says there is class struggle and Fascism says, *'they are to blame, those people there, others there.'*

Paul strikes down the three fake religions of the West, dead. In fact, they never lived. They are simply figments of your futile minds, your futility. The word of God is the answer to opiates of the mind and brings freedom from futility.

Freedom from *'them across the river'*

In the north of Japan, way up there, there is a tiny peninsula called Oga. I went there in search of monsters. The monster of Oga is a creature of foulness and violence, known for its brutality and for the fear he instills in the children of the desolate hamlets and towns in the north in the darkness and deep snows of winter.

These monsters are known for their large heads, and faces more like deeply set masks, with open, bulging eyes and sharp razor teeth, they often run around with long straw-like hair and large sharp knives seeking to slice and dice whomever they find wandering alone in the snow or in the deep forest.

The Namahage and I never met up, surprisingly enough, except at the train station where two of them stand watch over the tourists and locals going past. Many of these towns have stories and legends about these creatures whose fault only resided in the fact that they looked different from the locals.

The Namahage obviously had poor dental work and larger noses, and maybe eye trouble, perhaps they were short-sighted or had low iron levels, and probably came from across the river, or a different village, or even from another island or nation in the distant path and found their way from social exclusion to separation to myth, and horror stories to tell your kids late at night when they needed to stay indoors.

Most societies, even morally and spiritually bankrupt ones like ours find it necessary to create monsters that lurk across the river, or in the forest, or within our towns and cities that prey on the innocent and corrupt others. The church has been doing it for centuries. The herbalists and local remedy specialists of the Middle Ages were called witches and burnt at the stake, or drowned, but for some reason, the churches that were so concerned with expelling evil covered their cathedrals with goblins and ogres and demonic beings.

The witches were also women so their power and prestige in society challenged the corrupt church and social leadership. If they were not killing witches and Protestants, the Roman Catholic Church and the Orthodox were killing Jews, Europe's favorite target for religious and secular fascism.

It is strange that whilst the church held power for 1,000 years, society failed to develop, grow, evolve, or benefit more than a tiny section of society in the West. Why was that? Why was it that Weber could celebrate the Protestant work ethic as a virtue and the basis for western capitalism and yet Jewish entrepreneurism was widely condemned by the same church as pernicious and evil?

The descendants of those who burnt witches and kept the poor in poverty and exterminated indigenous peoples are now the ones in the church seeking to gather support for the new *'enemies of the people.'* Their brazen arrogance, stupidity, and corruption are astounding for they not only whitewash our histories but adamantly rehash the same old stories of the Western Namahage for domestic consumption.

European fascists, at some point, come for the Jews, they always have and always will and behind the rhetoric of abuse directed at women, minorities, the left or the right, these white supremacists hold tightly the old dream of reviving ancient hatreds.

I can sense it simmering under the surface as I surf the net and read the latest *'evangelical'* or *'conservative Christian'* views on gays and gendered minorities, or foreigners, or colonial history, or imperialism. These days 'conservative Christian' is code for *'racist white supremacist,'* and *'Christian values,'* means *'white values.'* None of it is Christian.

It is no surprise that these men and women who have no faith in Christ are trying to use Christian rhetoric to stave their inevitable oblivion to the dustbin of history and so they pretend to talk about a God they do not know and a Christ they do not believe in. Their ideal world is run by rich white men, with slaves and Asians knowing their place and women in the home

My guess is 80% of churchgoing Christians these days fall for it, and the reason they do is that do not read their Bible and they do pray, and they do not use the brains God gave them, nor listen to the Spirit all Christians receive upon faith. Their religious leaders manipulate them, lie to them, trick them, and con them, stirring up their fears and anxieties, and telling them that out there in the snow is the Namahage, with their sharp teeth and long knives, or the enemy could be Russia, or China, or Biden or transgender kids, just have a blank slate and fill in the name. Maybe they should read what Paul says in Ephesians 6: 12:

'For our struggle is not against flesh and blood, but against the rulers, against the authorities, against the powers of this dark world and against the spiritual forces of evil in the heavenly realms.'

Freedom from the mob

Standing for the truth when all are against you is a difficult thing to do. It is far easier to do what the mob tells you to do, or what most people do, find out which way the wind is blowing, and take it from there.

This is especially true in churches in the West. Since churches depend not upon sound business practices but upon a mixture of state subsidies, tax exemptions, and weekly payments from congregation members, priests, ministers, and pastors generally only preach what their congregations want to hear. There are words to describe this moral cowardice and spiritual bankruptcy, but I will not utter them here.

If churches were free of the chains of state protectionism, deprived of their charity status, and free to operate legally as businesses, they may find themselves in positions where they could preach the gospel of God's grace unhindered, without worrying about the mob, I mean the congregations.

Tens of thousands of good men and women in the church have had their careers and lives ruined because they preached from the Bible and offended one or more people who held the purse strings of their salary and had then dismissed. Church officers have no rights under the law, no right to join a union, or collectively bargain, and no rights at all, and so many thousands of families were sent to the street, destitute and poor.

The church courts are run by corrupt families and individuals, and they use church courts to destroy people they don't like. All these courts are illegal as they invent laws that don't exist, and none of them comes from the Bible but from the dark times when churches had the power to kill people or imprison them. There is only one law and that is the law of the state. Most church leaders are mediocre, weak-willed, socially awkward, spiritually corrupt individuals, who use their positions to advance themselves at the expense of others. It has been the same for centuries. The church is largely a derivative of the ruling class anyway, especially in the British and American empires. It is the religion of the establishment and money, and so the gospel of God's grace vanished long ago.

How does this play out in practice? Well, ministers would approach a text of scripture where Jesus or some prophet might say something controversial or admonish people. The minister would either dismiss the text out of hand or tell his congregation that these strong words did not apply to them because he knows that they are all God's people and all good Christians.

These harsh words would of course only apply to those outside, and he would list the sinners either by name or by class. It is a typical practice. It is common also to publicly denounce individual 'sinners' from the pulpit in front of the congregation. This happens a lot too these days. No minister, not even the Pope knows the heart of anyone aside from themselves and it is a bold assumption to make that the congregation is entirely composed of Christian people.

The Biblical approach is simply to apply the text as presented to the various classes of people present and make it clear who God is, who we are, and how God might be known. It is simple, but most ministers, priests, and pastors do not do it. They want to entertain their audience, stay on their good side, to tickle their ears, use an old Puritan expression, we might say play to their strengths and avoid anything that might upset them.

The mob was always present in the life of Jesus wrestling against him to pressure him to work for them. I can find two instances in the Gospels when Christ resisted the pressure of the mob and held his ground. In John 2: 23-5, after he cleared the temple, he knew the danger. John wrote:

'Now while he was in Jerusalem at the Passover Festival, many people saw the signs he was performing and believed in his name. But Jesus would not entrust himself to them, for he knew all people. He did not need any testimony about mankind, for he knew what was in each person.'

In John 6:14-15, the mob made its move a second time.

'After the people saw the sign Jesus performed, they began to say, "Surely this is the Prophet who is to come into the world." Jesus, knowing that they intended to come and make him king by force, withdrew again to a mountain by himself.'

The Christian minister, pastor, or teacher who stands for God is far and few between in the West. Most congregations these days are not interested in the good news of God's grace, or Jesus Christ. Fascist sympathies run deep. Or they want God to bless their material life or get caught up in some controversy. Most religious leaders don't have the courage to suffer anything more than a paper cut for Jesus, but he calls us all to take up our cross daily, deny ourselves and follow him, even at church, where we need to stand alone, with Christ, against the mob.

5   WE DO NOT WRESTLE AGAINST FLESH
AND BLOOD

What Mona Lisa and God have in common

The only war Christians are called to fight is a spiritual war, and this war is largely a conflict against unseen enemies. Paul writes in Ephesians 6: 12,

'For we wrestle not against flesh and blood, but against principalities, against powers, against the rulers of the darkness of this world, against spiritual wickedness in high places' (King James Version).

The danger for Christians is to do what many evangelicals do and ignore spiritual conflict entirely and misinterpret the atonement, or what many Pentecostals do, and run down the rabbit hole looking into things that we can neither know, or understand.

The best approach for a Christian is to go back to first principles and that is the Bible. The Bible is God's word to us today, it is God speaking to us, and through the text of the scriptures, we understand who God is, who we are, and how God might be known. These three questions are really what the Bible is concerned with answering, and the answer for all three finds fulfillment in the person and work of Jesus, who he is, and what he did.

Eternal life is to know God and Jesus Christ whom he sent. It begins now, not after our physical death, and we are led by the Spirit of God, enabling us to call God our Father. The focus of the scriptures is to enable a person to know God. The Bible does not intend, nor did it ever intend to answer every question posed by the human mind. The Bible is not a science textbook, nor is it a political manual for the Republican Party, nor is it a proof-text for the right to bear arms. At the center of scripture is God, and all of scripture points to God. He is the focus of the scriptures, and this is not surprising for it is in the Bible where God is fully and completely expressed

To use an example from art, take the beautiful painting of the Mona Lisa. She is the focus of the painting. People flock from around the world to see her. They long to look into her eyes, ponder her form, rejoice in her position, and reflect upon themselves and how watching this painting enables them to see themselves as well. This is what art critics do I suppose, or certainly, I do when I approach great works of art.

Now the Mona Lisa is a portrait, and she takes up most of the space on the canvass. When Leo was painting her, his focus was her, but he had to situate her in some context so there was at least some background. On her right, in the distance is a bridge with some arches, presumably made of stone, over a faint river, though it is difficult to see the depth of the water, which contrasts with the much larger and deeper, and bluer river that extends behind her to the left of the painting. There is a road behind her on her left and the river goes from left to right, extending to the heavens.

Sadly, the painting has undergone all kinds of controversies, much like God has. Critics have argued over the identity of the portrait, the gender of the Mona Lisa, the name of the bridge, the significance of the arches, the political ideology of the portrait, the name of the river, the location of the scene, and so on. These arguments, contests, and controversies have made experts wealthy over the centuries, through dozens of books, but at the end of the day, it is a remarkable painting of a woman, and she remains the focus of attention when people see the portrait.

God and Mona Lisa have a lot in common. The focus of the Bible is God. A true Christian, a genuine Christian might spend their whole life pondering God, his word, his Son, and his Spirit and still never fully reach that place where they could say *'I know it all.'*

Then we have the fake Christians, the pseudo-Christians, and those who hang around Christians who have no interest in God whatsoever but are fascinated by the peripheral, the marginal, the speculative, and the irrelevant. In this chapter, we will ponder one of the strangest verses in the New Testament. After telling us we don't wrestle against flesh and blood, Paul tells us that we wrestle against spiritual forces. One would expect that then he would give us more details about these spiritual forces, but he doesn't. He ignores it completely and returns to the great theme of the Bible, God. Why he does this, and what it means for spiritual war against those with whom we wrestle, we will ponder.

You cannot blame everything on Russia

It is a sign of a sterile political culture when imagination is lost. When Trump was elected in 2016, Russia was to blame. Everything Trump did meant he was Putin's puppet. It was 'Russia, Russia, Russia,' and even though the slurs, accusations, and allegations against Trump and Russia were hoaxes, Russophobia continued, even when Trump lost office and became citizen Trump. Now, everything that goes wrong in the world is blamed on Russia, from shortages in toilet paper to famine in Africa. Russia is to blame, it is their fault, and they are evil, says the morally bankrupt media and Congress.

As I said, a sterile culture exists when imagination is lost. One nation cannot be to blame for so much. It is simply impossible, and yet America cannot exist without the creation of an external Devil who acts to undermine their republic which was allegedly formed by God.

American political culture is a petri dish for the cultivation of fascism and has been churning out fascists for well over a century, from Billy Sunday to Donald Trump. Americans by their love of mixing religion and state together were simply continuing the nightmare of religious fascism that ruled the West for 1,000 years.

American Christians claim that their liberal society is based on God-given rights, but the Christian Bible does not agree. Point to me where it does. We do not wrestle against flesh and blood. This means that liberalism is false because individuals do not compete against one another. This means that Marxism is false because classes do not compete against one another. This means that Fascism is false because the problems in society are not caused by groups of people, rather they are caused by complex problems brought about by the logistical, organizational, and technological challenges of running a nation. Paul writes in Ephesians 6: 12,

'For we wrestle not against flesh and blood, but against principalities, against powers, against the rulers of the darkness of this world, against spiritual wickedness in high places.'

We do not wrestle against people. We do however wrestle *'against principalities, against powers, against the rulers of the darkness of this world, against spiritual wickedness in high places.'* In Greek, Paul is careful to articulate four times that we wrestle against someone. He repeats himself. This word in English 'against' is the Greek word pros which mean *'against'* and is mentioned in the New Testament over 700 times. There is no textual ambiguity in the use of Paul's word *'against.'* He is emphasizing the point, not to highlight the ones against whom we wrestle, but to emphasize the ones against whom we do not. In this verse, Paul repeats himself five times that we do not wrestle against flesh and blood. He might not survive a grammar check, but Paul is making a point that we need to understand. This means as Christians we do not wrestle against Russia, or China, or the Left, or socialists, or Biden, or Trump, or Putin, or gays, or women, or Mexican migrants, or anyone. These are the people fascists wrestle with, but not Christians.

Sad and pitiful are those Christians who follow fascism, they hear a little bit of Jesus in the rhetoric or a little bit of God in the speeches, but these fascists hate God, and they want you to hate the people they hate. You cannot be a fascist and a Christian. It is impossible. The slogan of fascism is a middle finger at the heavens, and it is tragic to see so many Christians lining up to unfurl the banners against the latest reason why America is falling into recession.

The fascists say that Russia is to blame for the economy, but that is false. The answer is easy: America printed trillions of dollars it did not have, and this pushed up inflation. If America spent fewer trillions on bombs and missiles and nuclear weapons, it would make fewer enemies in the world in the long run. But there are no greater supporters in America for the war economy than in the church, which is full of Christian fascists who seem to think that God's war is America's war and God's enemies are anyone who dares to challenge America. This is profound spiritual Satanic delusion. We do not wrestle against flesh and blood.

Unseen enemies

These days we are afflicted with all kinds of unseen enemies. We do not need to see something with the naked eye to realize that they are dangerous to our lives, loved ones, and community. Sometimes it is impossible to detect them and other times there are clear symptoms. Living in Post-Covid Hysteria, we now know of almost a dozen variants of the virus rampaging across the world, with the panoply of *'vaccines'* unable to staunch, protect, deflect, or eliminate the presence, impact, or transmission of the variants. Then there are all the other typical seasonal ailments and diseases that afflict people, and many of these are unseen. They do exist. Scientists convince us that they do and there are various remedies and treatments and therapeutics for them.

These unseen enemies have been with us for thousands of years, but it is only in the last century or so, that doctors and scientists have been able to accurately study them, fight them, and in many cases, sadly, replicate them in laboratories. Biological weapons have been used repeatedly since the First World War (1914-1918), and these involve the use of some of these unseen enemies as weapons of mass destruction. Paul writes in Ephesians 6: 12,

'For we wrestle not against flesh and blood, but against principalities, against powers, against the rulers of the darkness of this world, against spiritual wickedness in high places.'

We do not wrestle against people. We do however wrestle *'against principalities, against powers, against the rulers of the darkness of this world, against spiritual wickedness in high places.'*

Before we focus on the four unseen enemies, let us chart their effects or symptoms on the life of a Christian or a group of Christians. Let us look at the first two here. The first symptom of the effect of these unseen enemies is attraction towards error regarding God, the embracing of things that are not true (Ephesians 6: 14), that undermine our confidence in the identity and promises of God and his Son Jesus Christ.

This is not primarily about whether we lie or not, though deceit should not be part of the character of a Christian, but more about the truth concerning God. *'You can't believe that these days,'* for example, or *'science has disproved that,'* or *'Christianity is stupid people, only intelligent people are atheists,'* are some examples where this questioning might take place. In the absence of truth, there is ambiguity, and then error.

Many Christians seem to think that we live in a world of greyish hues, not white or black, but everyone else is very black or white, so why should Christians give up truth to appease their fundamentalist friends? The main attack on truth has to do with the person and work of Jesus Christ, and anything that Jesus said contradicts the current political conventional wisdom of the ruling classes.

The second effect or symptom on the life of a Christian or group of Christians concerns the nature of goodness or purity in God's sight. It is here it gets complicated because the New Testament clearly wants God's people to *'be holy as I am holy'* (1 Peter 1: 16), and the desire for the return of Christ one day encourages Christians to pursue purity (1 John 3: 3).

Personal holiness is not the grounds for salvation, and no one alive is good enough in terms of moral standing to stand before God alone, as God is perfect. Personal holiness is a derivative, a consequence of something supernatural in the life of a person where the holiness of another is, in a very real sense, shared with another, so that the righteousness or holiness of the first is the righteousness or holiness of the other.

It is here where so many Christians come unstuck. The Spirit is associated with righteousness and the Law is associated with sin. It is not us obeying the Law that makes us right with God. It is the work of Christ and his righteousness that becomes ours and the Spirit of Christ is given to us with righteousness itself. For some bizarre reason, most Christians do not like to talk to others about the righteousness of Christ they have received which makes them right with God. Instead, their entire focus is on their personal holiness and the failings of others to live up to their standards which are not very high because their salvation did not depend on anything they did in the first place or anything they could ever do in terms of personal holiness.

The symptom of illness in the Christian is not an unholy life. James says clearly that we all stumble in many ways all the time. The problem is forgetting or even removing in our minds and in our hearts the covering of the Lord's righteousness over us and standing before God outside of the embrace of Christ. If you stand before God without Christ's righteousness you will not be able to stand before the holiness of God. It is attacking the truth about Jesus, and it is the nature of righteousness that is the effects of the unseen enemies in the life of a Christian.

Spiritual sickness

Paul writes in Ephesians 6: 12,

'For we wrestle not against flesh and blood, but against principalities, against powers, against the rulers of the darkness of this world, against spiritual wickedness in high places.'

We do not wrestle against people. We do however wrestle *'against principalities, against powers, against the rulers of the darkness of this world, against spiritual wickedness in high places.'* Before we focus on the four unseen enemies, let us chart their effect, or symptoms on the life of a Christian or a group of Christians. The first two we looked at in the previous section. Now, the last four. The third symptom concerns the nature of the good news of God's grace (Ephesians 6: 15). It is when Christians stop talking about the good news and start talking about something else. Paul characterizes the gospel, or the good news as being a message of peace, peace with God. Do you hear this every Sunday? Of course not, the focus is morality, or personal holiness, or prosperity gospel, or the Culture War or the End Times or Revelation or America or demons, and so on.

The fourth symptom concerns the gnawing growth of cynicism and unbelief, which is perhaps the worst sign of a sick soul (Ephesians 6: 16). There is nothing worse than someone who has drawn near to God and then drawn back. Churches are full of these people, and so are religious schools, and seminaries, they have as the writer of the Hebrews notes in chapter 6: 4-6:

'It is impossible for those who have once been enlightened, who have tasted the heavenly gift, who have shared in the Holy Spirit, who have tasted the goodness of the word of God and the powers of the coming age and who have fallen away, to be brought back to repentance. To their loss they are crucifying the Son of God all over again and subjecting him to public disgrace.'

The author is writing of Jewish people before AD 70 (which is when it was written as it contains no admission of the destruction of the Temple), who sought to find the Messiah in Christ but turned away and saw at the cross of Christ only shame and ignominy, seeking then to return to the Old Covenant with God based on the Law and sacrifices. This had been overturned by Christ and his death on the cross.

While the original context has been lost, these verses still apply to so many who bathe themselves in the privileges of faith but ultimately live in unbelief and return to Sinai and self-effort. What happens is that they reject the Savior on the cross. Jesus means nothing to them and so they go back to the *'Temple at Jerusalem'* or their church and seek God's forgiveness through the Law of Moses. This is where most Christians end up, not at Golgotha and God's grace, but at Sinai and the untouchable mountain, a time of despair and sadness and inflexible holiness. It many ways it is not their fault as so many Christian ministers preach Moses more convincingly than they preach faith in Christ.

The fifth symptom concerns the erosion of assurance of salvation, or crumbling confidence in the promises of God concerning what God has promised us in Christ (Ephesians 6: 17). So many Christians languish with this illness, feel their guilt, and sin, and never feel forgiven, never accept their position before God and never find peace. It is not surprising, since the Orthodox and Catholics don't preach the Gospel and are not interested in ending guilt and shame because with the assurance of salvation, their money will dry up and their power over the people will end.

The final symptom is, in my mind, the one most at risk today and that is misunderstanding the identity and role of the Holy Spirit. This is seen in the erosion of confidence in the Bible as the Word of God. Many Christians do not have a problem with the Bible – they claim that its every word is infallible and inerrant and yet they are dissatisfied with it, spending much of their time speculating on questions the Bible does not pose or finding answers to questions the Bible does not ask.

It is this symptom that Paul seeks strongly to address in Ephesians 6: 12. What is he talking about and what is he careful to avoid? Sadly, many Christians love the Bible, but they are deeply impatient and unhappy with what they see as incomplete answers to the questions they ask. This illness drives them to seek solace online in the warm embrace of men and women who make everything up as they go along, making a fortune.

With whom do Christian struggle?

Paul writes in Ephesians 6: 12

'For we wrestle not against flesh and blood, but against principalities, against powers, against the rulers of the darkness of this world, against spiritual wickedness in high places.'

We do not wrestle against people. We do however wrestle *'against principalities, against powers, against the rulers of the darkness of this world, against spiritual wickedness in high places.'* Who are these four unseen enemies of Christ? The first group are the rulers (NIV, ESV). Others translate them as *'principalities,'* (for example, KJV), though the former seems to be more accurate. Some of the colloquial Bibles are too dramatic and they read like an episode from a Marvel comic.

The Greek is *'archas,'* which comes from archomai which means the beginning. Almost every time the word *'archas'* is used it is in reference to *'the beginning.'* It is used to mean a ruler or principality in other places (Luke 12: 11, Luke 20: 20; Romans 8: 38; 1 Corinthians 15: 24; Ephesians 1: 21; Ephesians 3: 10; Colossians 1: 16; Colossians 2: 10; Colossians 2: 15; Titus 3: 1; and Jude 6).

In most of these instances, the *'ruler'* is not a political office, but the intention is clearly to designate spiritual authority, often of those beings opposed to God. I suspect that there is an obvious link between both uses of the word, suggesting ancient power in the spiritual realm opposed to God. Beyond this, little is known.

The second group are the *'authorities,'* (NIV), or *'powers,'* (KJV). In Greek, it reads *'exousias.'* Like the rulers, the authorities are in the plural. In Greek, the word is broader and generally means *'authority'* in the way we use it such as *'he has authority over others,'* and so on. These spiritual authorities are also spiritual beings of various ranks or positions with authority in the unseen world. We are told nothing about them, beyond their name.

The third group are the *'powers of this world's darkness.'* The NIV calls it *'against the powers of this dark world.'* The ESV calls it *'against the cosmic powers over this present darkness,'* and the KJV calls it *'against the rulers of the darkness of this world.'* What Paul is saying here is completely consistent with the writings of John the Apostle, especially the letters. It is a general, canvas-sort of a statement like John makes and like the kinds of expressions Christ makes in the Gospels.

But unlike rulers and authorities, Paul uses an unlikely and little-used word in Greek *'kosmokratoras'* which is related to the word *'cosmos'* which is another word translated as the *'world'* in English. It is a noun and a person, so it is most likely to be a reference to Satan himself, Diabolos, and his rule of darkness over the world.

The fourth and final group are *'spiritual wickedness in the heavenly realms.'* The KJV renders it *'against spiritual wickedness in high places,'* the NIV renders it *'the spiritual forces of evil in the heavenly realms,'* and the ESV renders it *'the spiritual forces of evil in the heavenly places.'*

The word *'spiritual'* is essential for it is in Greek, coming from pneuma which is spirit or breath and that is beyond dispute. The word in dispute is *'heavenly realms,'* and this is in Greek *'epouraniois.'* This word is used often in the New Testament to mean *'heaven'* or *'the heavens,'* or *'heavenly things,'* but Paul tells us nothing beyond this general statement.

Paul is not outlining in detail the character of the spiritual world. Paul is writing to provide Christians with all that they need to know about those with whom we wrestle. He mentions them all in one verse, for his emphasis is not on the disease, but the cure, his emphasis is not on the problem but the solution. He cuts to the chase and does not dwell and what we do not need to know, and instead he goes to what it means to know God and be known by God which is the good news.

Reject the fake news of the unseen world

For some reason, fear of the Devil sells. People love to be terrified of demons, the End of the World, the Last Days, the names and positions of demons and spiritual beings, their history and genealogy, possession, whether there is one heaven or ten, the names of demons, virtually anything in the vast library that has become *'spiritual warfare.'* The online world is full of websites that are incredibly popular, but which are entire works of fiction, with fake pastors, ministers, and priests, inventing Bible verses, making up things, and writing what is essentially *'spiritual fiction,'* parading as Biblical truth.

Much of it are the anxieties of fascists in America, who are terrified that their holy nation of America, blessed by God, the greatest nation in the history of the world, and the lynchpin in God's plan of salvation in the Last Days, is under threat by the other 6.9 billion people who have the arrogance and sinfulness of wanting to live on the same planet. We need to reject the fake news of the unseen world. The apostles urged early Christians to avoid topics that were pointless, in other words, topics that led nowhere. Paul writes in 2 Timothy 2: 23:

'Don't have anything to do with foolish and stupid arguments, because you know they produce quarrels.'

In Titus 3: 9, he reiterates this advice:

'But avoid foolish controversies and genealogies and arguments and quarrels about the law, because these are unprofitable and useless.'

For some reason, the Christians whom Timothy served were always arguing about these things. Paul raises it twice. He argues in 1 Timothy 1: 3-5:

'As I urged you when I went into Macedonia, stay there in Ephesus so that you may command certain people not to teach false doctrines any longer or to devote themselves to myths and endless genealogies. Such things promote controversial speculations rather than advancing God's work—which is by faith. The goal of this command is love, which comes from a pure heart and a good conscience and a sincere faith.'

I can say with absolute certainty, and I too have the Spirit of God, that the ones who love to promote these myths and legends and talk of the unseen world, are not interested in *'advancing God's work, which is by faith,'* nor will they be people *'of love which comes from a pure heart and a good conscience and a sincere faith.'* Paul repeats himself in 1 Timothy 4: 7:

'Have nothing to do with godless myths and old wives' tales; rather, train yourself to be godly.'

For Paul, the decisive cosmic moment is not the *'Last Days,'* but the death and resurrection of Christ. This means that Paul and Christian Fascists must part company. Many of them are convinced that the big showdown against evil is yet to be played out in the Middle East involving Russia, Israel, and America. They see the death of Christ as a footnote that exists in a world that did not know the exceptionalism of America. For Paul, the cross is everything and it is the same for all Christians. He writes about this in Colossians 2: 8,

'See to it that no one takes you captive through hollow and deceptive philosophy, which depends on human tradition and the elemental spiritual forces of this world rather than on Christ.'

In verses 9-10, Paul outlines the authority and power of Christ constantly denied by fascists:

'For in Christ all the fullness of the Deity lives in bodily form, and in Christ you have been brought to fullness. He is the head over every power and authority.'

The fascists must denounce the Bible to advance their imbecilic American-centric mumbo jumbo of the Last Days. Paul says further in verses 13-15:

'When you were dead in your sins and in the uncircumcision of your flesh, God made you alive with Christ. He forgave us all our sins, having cancelled the charge of our legal indebtedness, which stood against us and condemned us; he has taken it away, nailing it to the cross. And having disarmed the powers and authorities, he made a public spectacle of them, triumphing over them by the cross.'

At the cross, Jesus defeated the rulers, the authorities, the Devil, and the spiritual wickedness in the heavens. We need to reject the fake news of the unseen world and accept the good news of the risen Lord Jesus Christ whose death changed the world, the spiritual world, and all in between.

Don't go down the rabbit hole

The temptation for Christians in Ephesians 6: 12 is to want to know more about the unseen world. Well, the Bible is silent on most of it, and so you will need to go down the rabbit hole of conspiracy and speculation, and this will take you further from the cross and the Lord Jesus Christ. For Paul and for us, the matter of first importance is what happened at the cross, 2000 years ago.

This is exactly what the author of the Hebrews is talking about in chapter 2 verse 14-18:

'Since the children have flesh and blood, he too shared in their humanity so that by his death he might break the power of him who holds the power of death—that is, the devil— and free those who all their lives were held in slavery by their fear of death. For surely it is not angels he helps, but Abraham's descendants. For this reason, he had to be made like them, fully human in every way, in order that he might become a merciful and faithful high priest in service to God, and that he might make atonement for the sins of the people. Because he himself suffered when he was tempted, he can help those who are being tempted.'

It is also what John says in 1 John 1: 7-9:

'Dear children, do not let anyone lead you astray. The one who does what is right is righteous, just as he is righteous. The one who does what is sinful is of the devil, because the devil has been sinning from the beginning. The reason the Son of God appeared was to destroy the devil's work.'

These verses deeply trouble the fascists who pore over Revelation for the latest sign and wonder to inject in their ever-expanding literature on the Last Days, the main hero America, the main villain, America's enemies which are led by the Devil, and the Savior of the world is America, America, God bless America.

For over a century this rubbish, this garbage, this fascist nonsense dominates American Christianity and is a disgrace. Not only does it bring the nation of America into disrepute, but it mocks Americans, and makes fun of them. If only Americans knew what Christian Fascists thought of them, maybe they do, and maybe the cat is out of the bag on that one. But if I want to shut them up for good – that is Christian Fascists in America – let us read what Paul wrote in Colossians 1: 15-20:

'The Son is the image of the invisible God, the firstborn over all creation. For in him all things were created: things in heaven and on earth, visible and invisible, whether thrones or powers or rulers or authorities; all things have been created through him and for him. He is before all things, and in him all things hold together. And he is the head

of the body, the church; he is the beginning and the firstborn from among the dead, so that in everything he might have the supremacy. For God was pleased to have all his fullness dwell in him, and through him to reconcile to himself all things, whether things on earth or things in heaven, by making peace through his blood, shed on the cross.'

Finally, Philippians 2: 5 -11:

'In your relationships with one another, have the same mindset as Christ Jesus: Who, being in very nature God, did not consider equality with God something to be used to his own advantage; rather, he made himself nothing by taking the very nature of a servant, being made in human likeness. And being found in appearance as a man, he humbled himself by becoming obedient to death—even death on a cross! Therefore, God exalted him to the highest place and gave him the name that is above every name, that at the name of Jesus every knee should bow, in heaven and on earth and under the earth, and every tongue acknowledge that Jesus Christ is Lord, to the glory of God the Father.'

Paul does not dwell much on the nature of spiritual beings because the key historical event is the death, resurrection, and exaltation of the Lord Jesus Christ. Don't go down the rabbit hole. Follow Jesus instead. What is that laughter I hear? Ah yes, it is all these fake ministers, priests, and pastors online laughing all the way to the bank. Don't worry, they will keep the fear rolling in as you keep coughing up the dough. After all, the last thing they want you to do is to open your Bible.

6   IS GOD A REPUBLICAN?

Is God against the Left?

Recently, one of the most prominent American Christian Fascists made a statement in public that was widely welcomed and applauded by many Christians in America. In fact, he received a standing ovation from the crowd, and many see this fascist as a future President of America.

It was, however, completely repugnant, deeply offensive, utterly wrong, and should have been widely and immediately condemned by the American Christian community. That it was not, is indicative of the cancer of Christian Fascism that plagues Christianity in America, a sign of a nation where God has his face turned away. Like so many of us, the revolting hypocrisy of the church in America sickens God.

God is not against the Left, and he is not against the Right. He is not on anyone's side. What this man boasted goes beyond anything Donald Trump ever said. If you were concerned about Donald's Christian Fascism, then you should be absolutely horrified with Ron's.

Ron, I will say this, and I will say this to the one who stood up and deliberately misquoted the Bible in his re-election campaign. I have seen men and women in the pulpit get excited with their sermon or their talk and they say things that they should not, or they go too far, in the heat of the moment It is a temptation for public speakers especially when they venture into extemporary speech. That is natural and I think that most people would understand this. But, in my research, you have used these lines more than once. I may be incorrect, but not according to the news reports that seem to be readily available. These are scripted alterations.

They are public statements. Correct me if I am wrong. I am only going on public reports.

No Christian would ever think of doing what you did. John the apostle warns us of a curse if we add or take away from the text of the Bible (Revelations 22:18-19). Liberal Christians might deny the authenticity of the Bible, but they respect the text and will say that certain verses are metaphorical, or allegorical. No follower of the Lord Jesus Christ would tamper with the text the way you did. In my whole life, I have not witnessed, the deliberate and public corruption of a clear Biblical text. During Covid Hysteria, many Christian Fascists misapplied Moses' rules on loving others to the vaccine, but they correctly quoted the Bible.

Ron, you have in that sentence revealed the heart and the evil of Christian Fascism. Christian Fascism is a clear and present danger to the health of any nation. Let us look at the verses you lied about. They come from Ephesians 6: 11-17:

'Put on the full armor of God, so that you can take your stand against the devil's schemes. For our struggle is not against flesh and blood, but against the rulers, against the authorities, against the powers of this dark world and against the spiritual forces of evil in the heavenly realms. Therefore, put on the full armor of God, so that when the day of evil comes, you may be able to stand your ground, and after you have done everything, to stand. Stand firm then, with the belt of truth buckled around your waist, with the breastplate of righteousness in place, and with your feet fitted with the readiness that comes from the gospel of peace. In addition to all this, take up the shield of faith, with which you can extinguish all the flaming arrows of the evil one. Take the helmet of salvation and the sword of the Spirit, which is the word of God.'

Ron however deliberately tampered with the text of the Bible for his own political purposes. He said on one occasion on 23 July:

'You gotta be ready for battle. So put on the full armor of God. Take a stand against the left's schemes. Stand firm with the belt of truth buckled around your waist. Will you face fire from flaming arrows, but the shield of faith will protect you.'

We do not struggle against flesh and blood Ron. It is Diabolos, and we stand because of the Lord Jesus Christ, whom you didn't mention because you are not a Christian, but a fascist, and the proof is your deliberate, deceitful twisting of God's word for your own sordid political gains. There are lots of people in America who hate Christians for all sorts of reasons, but most of them refuse to twist the Bible to make cheap political shots, though they often point to the Bible to highlight religious hypocrisy, and so they should.

The greatest tragedy of course is the mad American Christians who think Ron is right and that God is wrong. They will make their stand against the Left without Christ because they don't need him, they have Trump, they have Ron, they have their conservative Supreme Court Judges and their Constitution, but they will most certainly fall, for only in Christ can a person stand against Diabolos and his schemes. He is probably sitting in one of his favorite churches today, chuckling and why wouldn't he?

Reading the Bible means paying attention

Whenever you learn a new language, a literal language, or a language relating to your work culture, you need to pay attention to the detail. Words are important, as well as how words fit together, how words can be used, how they should not be used, and how they can be flexible or inflexible. Every language has its own rules and conventions, and detail is everything.

The Bible is no different. Today, in the English language, there are well over fifty versions. Most are good and reliable. Bible translators, overall, have done a remarkable job in translating both the meaning as well as the sense of words. The Bible was not written in English but in New Testament Greek, Hebrew, and a little Aramaic. These are ancient languages and have exercised a profound influence on many languages used today.

At Seminary, I studied both Hebrew and New Testament Greek, and in my Freedom Matters Today writings, I am always returning to the original texts for their meanings, nuances, and contexts. It is essential for me as I am trying to accurately teach or divide the Word of God. Please don't take my word for it. Test everything by the text of scripture. We need to pay attention or things get lost in translation, as they say.

Many of the stricter English versions (such as NIV, NASB, RSV, ESV), of the Bible, usually follow the Greek and Hebrew intent, in other words, they add very little in terms of the meanings, with few embellishments or flourishing. They are reliable and anyone can read them and have confidence that they are reading texts that have, overall, been accurately translated. The Wycliff Bible Translators, for example, do an incredible job translating the Bible into many languages which do not yet, have a Bible in their language. It is astounding to think that even in the current century, many people cannot read the Bible in the words they use every day.

What this all means is that we need to pay attention when we read the Bible. There are several principles that might be useful. The first is that repetition suggests something highly significant. In other words: listen carefully.

All the words of the Bible are significant but when a writer repeats himself, it suggests clearly that he wants us to pay attention. For example, in Romans 13, Paul tells Christians twice that they should pay tax to Caesar – and that includes *'churches'* as there were no tax exemptions in the first century. He emphasizes what the church likes to ignore.

Psalm 19 uses multiple images and ideas to convey the same idea, that God's word is truth, it is like honey, it is like gold, it is like the brightness of the sun. The Psalmist is talking about the Law of God. By the end of the Psalm, you get the point. In Ephesians 6 verses 11 and 13, the apostle Paul tells his readers twice to *'put on the armor of God.'* In other words, he emphasizes the importance of this action in the life of a Christian.

The second principle is that grammar matters and, conjunctions, which are words that connect things such as *'but,'* or *'therefore,'* or *'and,'* or *'yet.'* There is nothing more important when reading the Bible than to pay attention to the way these conjunctions are used. Paul uses them frequently in his style of writing such as Ephesians 2: 4, Romans 5:8, and Ephesians 6: 13 which reads

'Therefore put on the full armor of God, so that when the day of evil comes, you may be able to stand your ground, and after you have done everything, to stand.'

Finally, do the author credit and read what he is saying. Don't put words in his mouth, take things out of context, or add or subtract words. Try to grasp the meaning of the sentence, and in reading, see words in their context, and let the words speak for themselves, in the way they are meant to be read. Look at the sentence, look at the words, see how they relate to each other, and respect them. Let language speak. Pay attention.

The only armor God wants you to wear

In Australia and other Commonwealth nations, there is one sport that rules all others. It is quintessentially English and is a relic of empire. Nonetheless, it is exalted, respected, and adored by millions, regardless of the appalling way the British ruled their part of the world, or what used to be their part of the world. Cricket is not a safe sport.

Indeed, it is one of the deadlier sports, and as a result, players need to wear body armor to protect themselves from the ball. Armor is typically worn on the shins, over the groin, with a helmet and face guard. This was not always the case.

In the 1932-3 Ashes competition between England and Australia, the English Captain Douglas Jardine implemented his infamous *'bodyline'* strategy, which effectively targets the batsmen directly. At the time it causes an outcry and an uproar and was a PR disaster for the English. Bert Oldfield, an Australian batsman, was struck on the head, causing a fracture. Today, cricketers dress like Japanese samurai when they go onto the field, though they carry no weapons, and they play a sport in relative safety.

The armor a Christian is to wear is essentially to acquaint themselves clearly with their new identity in Christ, coming to terms with their relationship with God, and who they are in relation to him. God's armor is not something external to the Christian. It is not literally armor, like the cricket pads and helmet, but they are images that convey substantial information about identity, relationship, and responsibility. Paul writes in Ephesians 6: 13:

'Therefore, put on the full armor of God, so that when the day of evil comes, you may be able to stand your ground, and after you have done everything, to stand.'

Paul is repeating himself. He said the same in verse 11: *'put on the full armor of God.'* It is emphasis. It is essential. Armor implies conflict, not a walk in the park, it implies war, not peace. Being a Christian means being ready to fight, be prepared for action, and being aware of the danger.

The second principle is the conjunction in English 'therefore,' though it is a preposition in Greek, *'dia'* which means *'through,' 'on account of'*, or *'because of.'* The word is used because of the preceding verses which explain that our adversaries are not human, but spiritual forces of evil. Those who claim that Christians struggle against socialists or capitalists or Left or Right are not following Jesus Christ, they are twisting the Bible to suit their own political agenda. Verse 12 is very clear in providing the context for verse 13:

'For our struggle is not against flesh and blood, but against the rulers, against the authorities, against the powers of this dark world and against the spiritual forces of evil in the heavenly realms.'

The only armor that will enable to stand against Diabolos is God's armor – not the arguments of the Constitution, or *'Christian Heritage,'* or

Trump, or DeSantis, but God himself. Jesus stood against Diabolos so we can stand with him and not stand alone, for if we stood alone, we would fall. The third principle that we discovered yesterday is to read the full sentence It reads:

'Therefore, put on the full armor of God, so that when the day of evil comes, you may be able to stand your ground, and after you have done everything, to stand.'

The only war Christians are to fight

When the Russians declared war on the American puppet regime of Ukraine, Western troops were still being withdrawn from Afghanistan. The Twenty-Years War resulted in American failure to unseat the Taliban. Western Christian leaders fell over themselves in their enthusiasm to condemn Russia's actions in Ukraine as evil, illegal, and criminal. They said nothing about Afghanistan. Their many religious businesses are divesting themselves of anything linked to Russia and some use the pulpits to condemn Putin as the latest Anti-Christ.

How quickly they forget American foreign policy and the greatest warmongering nation in the last century, America. America can have 300-plus military bases around the world and there is silence, but when China proposes one base in some obscure Pacific nation, the West has apoplexy and Christian Fascists have a collective stroke.

Americans condemn the Chinese Communist Party for writing their own version of the Bible to remove foreign influences. I have not seen the text, but I do know that chapels and church buildings and Western values are found nowhere in Holy Scripture, nor were the Bible texts written in English, so cultural sensitivity is important and has been sadly missing in evangelism for the last century or so.

China's heavy-handed reaction needs to be seen in the context of a history of fake versions of Christianity going right back to the Taiping Rebellion. They have every right to fear Western-inspired corrupt versions of Christianity, that have no basis in the Bible but are simple vehicles for promoting Western individualism.

But when an American leader misquotes the Bible, church leaders say nothing. Instead, they give him a standing ovation, and Christian fascists see this man as a new Trump, a new Savior to rescue the West. This hypocrite said,

'You gotta be ready for battle. So put on the full armor of God. Take a

stand against the left's schemes. Stand firm with the belt of truth buckled around your waist. Will you face fire from flaming arrows, but the shield of faith will protect you.'

This is something the Soviets or Maoists might have said in the glory days of the 1960s but that an American leader would utter these words is absolutely astounding. It shows how deep, and dangerous Christian Fascism has become in the West.

It is as mad as the *'Q'* nonsense during the Trump years, the proposition that there were goodies in the American army fighting the deep state and wanting to drain the swamp. Q supporters curiously did not support the release of Julian Assange, nor would they countenance the allegations made against American conduct in the Middle East.

Most men and women employed in the armed services of every country on the planet conduct themselves according to the rules of engagement. Nowhere does the Bible prohibit people from enlisting, but as I have said before, God does not take sides in war. He respects the day, and the conduct of war, and the ultimate purpose of all things is hidden in his counsel.

If God is on our side in this war, then he effectively murders those who die in battle, and I cannot accept that. Soldiering may be evolving towards automation, but people are still people, and God respects the choices we make, even on the battlefield.

Christians like to say that *'there are no atheists in a foxhole,'* but so what? God is opposed to human conflict as it is rooted in sin. You fight alone in war. Fascists like to talk about the 1914 Christmas Day lull on the Western Front between the English and German troops, but again, so what? Christians fought and slaughtered each other in pointless battles that achieved nothing. The best the corrupt Western Church could muster was one day of peace in years of butchery, human depravity, and mass killing. What side was God on in your American Civil War? How about the War of Independence? In both conflicts, both sides were nominally Christian.

The nonsense of the Q conspiracy, the silence on Julian Assange, the warmongering culture of America, the military-industrial complex, the Culture War, and Christian Fascism have all muddied the waters, and they have confused a lot of people. It is time to end this confusion by returning to the Bible and the only war, Christians are to fight, the war against spiritual evil. Our enemies are not flesh and blood. Paul tells us:

'Therefore, put on the full armor of God, so that when the day of evil comes, you may be able to stand your ground, and after you have done everything, to stand.'

This is the only war Christians are to fight.

They don't come in the dark

The Bible records that when angels turn up, people feel a deep sense of fear and foreboding. This is, as the New and Hebrew Testaments testify, the normal way these messengers of God do his work amongst us. The shepherds at the advent of the birth of Jesus (Luke 2: 10), Gabriel's appearance to Zechariah (Luke 1: 13), and his appearance before Mary (Luke 1: 30) for example, all indicate that angels instill in people a sense of fear.

By contrast, Diabolos is described as a friendly, approachable being that sits easily in our world. He is described as a serpent in Genesis 3, simply one of the many animals God had created in the garden. In Job, Diabolos simply pops in for a chat with Yahweh in the heavenly council. Paul describes the Devil as one masquerading as an angel of light (2 Corinthians 11:14). Put simply, angels put the fear of God into people, whereas the Devil pulls up a chair and claims to be your friend. This is not the way many Christians have understood the way evil works.

This is confirmed in the life of Jesus. Churches are sometimes seen as places of safety, but the Bible describes them as both often dangerous and opposed to God. Paul's lists of sins and transgressions in his letters do not apply to those who do not know Jesus, but to those who claim to follow him (Ephesians 4: 22-5; Colossians 2: 16-23). None of the seven assemblies listed in the first few chapters of John's Revelation survive unscathed by Christ. During our Lord's earthly ministry, synagogues were places where those oppressed by demons lived without contest or challenge (Mark 1: 21-6; Luke 4: 33). Church-going people in Nazareth also tried to murder Jesus by throwing him off a cliff (Luke 4: 29). The synagogues were created by the Pharisees, who conspired to murder Jesus because he did good to others. Paul tells the Ephesians in 6: 13 to:

'Therefore, put on the full armor of God, so that when the day of evil comes, you may be able to stand your ground, and after you have done everything, to stand.'

Christians are not to wait for the night, but for the day, they are to be prepared for the attack when they least expect it, for this *'day of evil.'* In Greek, this simply means a day, a 24-hour period, he is not describing a length of time or a lifetime, but a day, it is as simple as that. What Paul is saying is that at some point in life, on an ordinary day, Christians will be attacked spiritually, and it will be a surprise attack for they will not come at night. It is because they follow Jesus. It is because they are united to Christ by faith, their citizenship is in heaven and their Father is God.

On this day, on this ordinary day, their faith, trust, their allegiance, and their relationship with God will be contested. How, and in what form this will take, Paul does not tell us, but he does us that it will happen. Elsewhere Paul calls all days as evil (Ephesians 5: 16). By this he means simply that the world lives in a life of wickedness and has for a long time. This is a great comfort for Christians because it means that the world does not get better or worse, it simply is. This is great discomfort for fascists because, for them, the past was better than the present.

Christians are encouraged in this verse to stand, which means to stand their ground, which means to have their feet on the ground, planted, sure, and secure. They are also encouraged to prepare for the day ahead. Jesus tells us to ask the Father for *'our daily bread'* (Matthew 6: 11). The writer to the Hebrews tells us in 3: 13:

'But encourage one another daily, as long as it is called "Today," so that none of you may be hardened by sin's deceitfulness.'

Jesus also tells us not to worry about tomorrow but keep our minds and hearts focused on today.

'Therefore, do not worry about tomorrow, for tomorrow will worry about itself. Each day has enough trouble of its own.' (Matthew 6: 34).

The guidebook for the Christian today is not the writings of a politician or political party. We need to be aware of those who come in the day, with a smile and handshake. Will they accept Paul's argument, or will they close the Bible and tell you to follow them?

The hidden weapon in God's armor

From 1549 to 1637, Christianity flourished in Japan. From the late fifteenth century till the late nineteenth century, Christians were persecuted to the point of complete annihilation. From 1600 until the 1860s, many thousands of Christians kept their faith secret, many of them being crucified, burnt alive, drowned, or boiled alive if they were caught. The stories of their suffering are unique in the sense that they are not affected by the same hagiographical damage that afflicts Western accounts of sectarian martyrdom, especially between Roman Catholics and

European Protestants.

These stories are astounding, and these records are readily available. The martyrs were sometimes priests, both European and Japanese, but overall, most were ordinary people who decided to follow Jesus Christ no matter the cost. They were, overall, poor people, or farmers, though there were many in the samurai class who also converted.

How on earth could these people survive such terrible persecution? The final rebellion of Christians against the Japanese state occurred in 1637 which concluded in the brutal massacre of all survivors, up to 37,000 Christians. Perhaps in some way, Paul gives us the answer, or one answer in Ephesians 6: 13.

'Therefore, put on the full armor of God so that when the day of evil comes you may be able to stand your ground and after you have done everything, to stand.'

For Christians, God is their armor, and God has no favorites, all are treated the same by him. This may not be the message you hear in church, but I don't expect many churches these days to even bother opening their Bible, let alone following it. All Christians are the same in God's eyes, he does not look at the rich differently, nor is there a special place in his heart for the wealthy or those who live in the right suburbs or go to the best schools. If you put on the armor of God, says Paul, all of you, regardless of who you are, will be able to stand against the Devil.

The words we translate in English are quite remarkable, for they are perhaps words that we do not use as often as we should. These words in the NIV are *'you may be able.'* Some translate it as *'you will be able,'* but if you look at all the translations side by side, virtually all of them use the same words.

You may be able. In other words, you can. In other words, you are able. In order words, there can be victory. In other words, defeat is not inevitable. Diabolos through his discouragers, whom there are many, and no doubt, you have met them in your life as I have in mine, and they use four other words: *'it can't be done.'* But Paul responds with four words of hope, decisiveness, and action: *'you may be able.'*

The English phrase comes from the Greek verb dynēthēte which comes from the Greek word dunamai which means to be able, to have power. It is where we get our word dynamite, or dynamo. It is about power or ability. It is about God's power and God's ability. It is not about our power or our ability. It is God's armor we are to put on and those who do so, have the power to resist the temptations of the Devil.

This is what makes Ron DeSantis' rewriting of Ephesians 6 so pernicious and evil from a Christian perspective. He argues that we do not struggle against the Devil but against people. He argues that our enemy are our political opponents in an election campaign, which is a sordid and corrupt argument, alleging that he is God's warrior fighting for God against evil, which is hubris. He also argues that it is his political philosophy that will be able to stand against evil, which is complete and utter rubbish. If Liberalism stands against Diabolos, it will fall. All philosophies do.

No Christian fights against flesh and blood, the schemes are the Devils, the armor is Gods, and all people can put it on, and that is all people. This includes Democrats, it includes Biden, it includes Socialists, it includes people who have different political views to Ron DeSantis. Anyone with God's armor may be able to stand. This is God's hidden weapon. It is true power for all people who seek to stand with Christ.

The only war posture for Christians is defense

One of the strangest movies I have seen is the Princess Bride, based on the popular book, which I have, but have not read, by William Goldman. It challenged the way I saw movies and books concerning the existence and future of evil. In the movie, the main villain survives to live another day, while the princess is rescued by the hero and life goes on. There is no final battle with swords clashing, or a big punch up or a shootout.

Most other films of my generation in that genre end with such a climax, especially American films. There is a contest between good and evil and evil always ends up dead. Does the evil prince change his ways? Probably not. I do not know, but in the story, it doesn't matter, as his evil is staunched, and he is forced to retreat.

In the Christian war, the only posture is one of defense. The Christian is not to attack but to defend, to stand their ground, against evil. This goes against the grain; it is certainly against contemporary Christian politics which defines itself as a continual war against God's enemies in society. Christian Fascists have their *'hit list'* or *'kill list'* if we want to use this terminology and it includes everyone on the other side of their political philosophy. The Christian doesn't go to kill anyone. The Christian defends, the Christian deflects and the Christian defeats the attacks of spiritual wickedness. Paul writes in Ephesians 6: 13:

'Therefore, put on the full armor of God, so that when the day of evil comes, you may be able to stand your ground, and after you have done everything, to stand.'

Paul does not say:

'Put on the full armor of God so that when the radical left appears with their woke agenda, their critical race theory, and their liberal views, you can attack them and destroy them with the Constitution of America and the conservative supreme court judges.'

The Christian life has nothing to do with politics. The ones who claim that it does are Christian Nationalists or Fascists are easy to identify. They don't like the Bible; they don't like Jesus Christ and they don't like talking about their own faith because they don't have any. Paul is not talking about politics but everyday life, where most people live. Christianity is lived out in our lives with others and our lives with our own hearts. It is in the mind and in our social interaction where most of our experiences are created and it is these encounters Paul has in his mind.

This defensive position of the Christian is to stand your ground and when it is finished or accomplished, to continue standing. The position is one of defense to deflect the arrows or darts of the Devil and his followers and to stand once the dust has settled.

The words *'to stand your ground'* comes from the Greek verb *'antistēnai.'* Which means to withstand or stand against. It is where we get our word antihistamine, which are drugs to enable us to withstand diseases or illnesses. Paul's thinking on the armor of God is completely consistent with the New Testament. Jesus urges us not to swear by heaven or earth or make oaths but simply let our *'yes'* be *'yes'* and our *'no'* be *'no'* (Matthew 5: 33). Paul urges us not to take revenge on anyone and leave vengeance in the hands of God (Romans 12: 19).

Jesus urges his followers to love their enemies and do good to them (Matthew 5: 43-8). The fruit of the Holy Spirit is the opposite of the spirit of the world. In Galatians 5: 22-3, Paul tells us,

'But the fruit of the Spirit is love, joy, peace, forbearance, kindness, goodness, faithfulness, gentleness and self-control.'

Indeed, those bent on war and attack and defeating their political enemies cannot be followers of Christ. There is no room for God in their hearts, as they are too busy hating other people. As Paul says in Philippians 4: 8:

'Finally, brothers and sisters, whatever is true, whatever is noble, whatever is right, whatever is pure, whatever is lovely, whatever is

admirable—if anything is excellent or praiseworthy—think about such things.'

This state of mind is only possible for those who stand their ground against spiritual evil. Christians defend themselves with the armor of God and leave everything else to him. If we don't, we are not fighting God's war, but our own, and we fight alone.

7   FOLLOWING JESUS WHEN THE CHURCH HAS LOST ITS WAY

Following Jesus is true freedom

Following Jesus is the path to true freedom. At *Freedom Matters Today*, we look at freedom from a Christian perspective. We are not interested in politics but in the risen Lord Jesus Christ whom we seek to follow each day, not only Sunday morning at *'church.' Freedom Matters Today* is for victims and outcasts, searchers, and seekers. We reach out to those abused by the church and cast out, those who love Jesus but hate the church, and those who are interested in Jesus but offended by the church. *Freedom Matters Today* is for you.

How do we follow Jesus when the church has lost its way? How do we follow Jesus when the church has lost its way? Simple. Listen to what he says when no one else does. What Jesus says is found in the New Testament, in the Bible, mainly in the four Gospel accounts of his life and work – Matthew, Mark, Luke, and John. They each provide different perspectives on the life of Jesus, though much common ground exists between all of them.

What Jesus says and what he did are transformative, subversive, radical, and beautiful. For two thousand years, most of the church has spent its time trying to ignore him, while building their kingdoms on earth, murdering people who didn't submit to their usurped political power, and closing their Bibles. If only the church followed Jesus, it would not have lost its way.

Today, the church has lost its way. These days, the Western church is in such a dreadful state, that we really need to go back to basics. We need a simplicity of faith, a freedom that can only be found in the life, words, and work of Jesus Christ. We need freedom, true freedom that does not come from the government or the law, but from God, a gift of his presence and love, freedom to choose, freedom to love, and freedom to exist. Most churches are either places with a toxic culture and spiritual abuse or corrupt institutions that prey on the naïve for financial gain. That is part of the reason we say at Freedom Matters Today:

'don't go to church, follow Jesus instead.'

Churches are no longer safe places if they ever were in the first place. Trying to find a safe church is like the lottery, you might get lucky, but usually the house wins, and you leave with your heart broken and your pockets empty. If Christians followed the one, they call Jesus, apparently their Lord and Savior, the reputation of Christianity would be completely different.

How did the church lose its way and stop following Jesus? Let's start with the heart of Western Christianity, America. Christian Fascists in America have so twisted the Bible to suit their faith in America that they disrespect the flag and the nation on one hand, and on the other, they have lost their way. But first, some historical context.

Under the Obama-Biden regime, America facilitated the rise of Iran as a nuclear power in the Middle East. Hilary Clinton was supposed to be elected in 2016 and aside from going to war with Russia, the Iran nuclear deal was expected to continue. The Trump/Pence regime however rebelled and pushed back on war with Russia and the Iran deal, pursuing trade deals that resulted in the so-called Abraham Accords, largely dismissed by the media in America which is now almost entirely committed to the doctrine of Endless War and the profligate printing of money that has led to inflation.

Trump's policies undermined the political and economic forces that have shaped and benefited from American foreign policy since 9/11. The Biden/Harris regime has returned America to the status quo and led America to war with Russia, starting WW3. Biden is adored by the press and the bomb makers, both of whom benefit wonderfully from conflict. Biden is just the face, and one of the authors of the old regime that sought to reshape the world in America's image so it will be the only power in the world. Museums are full of relics from nations that also thought the same way.

American foreign policy is not *'Christian'*, it is strategic. Critical to America's strategic interests include the necessity of guaranteeing access to oil and other resources and as a direct consequence, America also supports Saudi Arabia and other Arab oil-producing nations. America has also helped to bankroll the Saudi war against Yemen, a complicated and confusing conflict that is virtually ignored by the West while it weeps crocodile tears for Ukraine. This American military support is considerable, strategic, and ongoing.

American support represents unquestionable loyalty to the Saudi royal family. It concerns strategic access to and control of oil reserves and other minerals. The goal is to sustain the economic and political power of the ruling class in America and the West. America, like all nations, behaves in a strategic manner to promote its interests abroad. I am not passing judgment on any of these foreign policies. It is the way of things and will not change, regardless of who is in power.

Jesus told us that right up to his return there will be wars and rumors of wars, so there will always be war, and war is hell, there is no right or wrong, and no one ever wins, except those who make the bombs and report the news. Christians have, overall, forgotten the words of Jesus and spend more time listening to politicians than they do praying to God. During the last year, few Christian leaders pray for peace. Rather, they support war with Russia and all the while ignoring the return to militarism in the two great fascist nations that caused the last war, Germany, and Japan. The churches didn't pray for peace last time, except for the many Japanese pacifists not imprisoned but praying in the Nagasaki Cathedral the day the Americans dropped the atomic bomb.

These policies to prop up Saudi Arabia are part of American foreign policy in the Middle East. Both Iran and the Saudis are enemies of Israel. Both would be happy if Israel did not exist, and both believe that Israel is an existential threat. America supports both sides, Israel, and anti-Israel, as it always has. It is a classic divide-and-rule policy. The British used it in Africa and Asia when they had their empire.

Democracy and freedom, America's Fake News

The Ukrainian people will pay for the trillions of dollars in reconstruction and military hardware acquisition, which will most likely leave Ukraine as a bankrupt, divided, and weakened nation squashed between NATO expansionism and Russian nationalism.

Millions will suffer the terrible consequences of war well into the third and fourth generations. The hatred between Russia and Ukraine will never die, but fester, and flourish, and this bile, malice, and wickedness will lead to the destruction of families, lives, and futures. Such is the face of all war. Those who expect the Irish to forget the ignominy of Britain or the Indians the rape of the subcontinent, or the Muslims the destruction of the Middle

East are living in a world of illusion. The West has sown hatred, chaos, and destruction, and its legacy is body bags, cemeteries, and death. The church, for its part, was a willing participant happy to forfeit faith in return for political and economic power.

The longer the war continues, the more accentuated and structural this misery will be. Poverty will be the future of Ukraine, suffering its language, and regret, its lasting memory. Soon the West will forget. It is what they do when they get bored, and Ukraine will be left alone, along with all the other nations cast aside by America when priorities change.

During America's war on Russia via Ukraine, the Americans have said this is a war between democracy and autocracy. The use of the word autocrat is deliberate. It is an ideological term and means nothing in practice. Ukraine is a fascist state or neo-fascist state, like Hungary or Poland these days. Ukraine is not remotely a democracy. It is a puppet regime run from Washington, after all, the Americans effected a coup in 2014 and have used Ukraine to provoke a war with Russia.

America and the West do not care about the Ukrainian people. They care about strategic policy as well as selling arms, which they have done successfully in the last year. Business has been booming, especially in bombs, mines, missiles, tanks, technology, bullets, and blank cheques from Congress. On the ground, there is no freedom or democracy in Ukraine. Russian Orthodox ritualists are being persecuted, as is anyone who dares to preach the gospel of peace that Christ proclaimed. Most of the opposition parties in Ukraine are persecuted.

Ukraine's foreign policy looks increasingly Stalinist, including calls to ban Russian culture and movement of people worldwide and reports that lists of foreign influencers who criticize Ukraine are to be assassinated. This is Pinochet and Chile all over again, except in Eastern Europe. Certainly, in the West, Russophobia is well underway. What are America's objectives in Ukraine? It is certainly not democracy.

It is bizarre that Biden and his cheerleaders condemn autocracy. America is an autocratic society. Both political parties aspire for absolute power and if they could, they would exterminate each other. They have a President whom they elect, and he is basically a kind of autocratic leader.

The US Constitution without Congress promotes an absolute dictator, like a King if you like, and America's regime is simply a secular version of the British monarchy and parliament. Yes, they copied the British. Yes, he is elected (no President has yet been a woman) for a maximum of 8 years but that might change in the future when they get rid of their antiquated Constitution. A similar system exists in Australia, New Zealand, and Canada, so-called *constitutional monarchies* where Governor Generals represent the British Monarch whose power and crown are never challenged.

The elites hate democracy and despise ordinary people, and we call this Liberalism. If we are to oppose autocracy, then why do we support Saudi Arabia? The answer of course is that the American ruling class and their surrogates and patrons don't bother even lying effectively anymore, such is the crisis in the American state. America supports autocrats and props up dictators and authoritarian regimes all the time.

This is essential for ensuring global stability and American prosperity. This *'acceptable hypocrisy'* is the lifeblood of Western democracy. It is one of the reasons the West is implacably hated by most of the world. What the West claims to believe in and their real intentions are completely different. The Bible calls this a sin. For some reason, America feels it must lie about what it does in the world. Previous empires didn't bother. Might was right. At least they were honest. Democracy, on the other hand, needs a culture of deceit, and a web of justifications to cover the basic functions of the state.

At this point, much of this is moot. I cannot change a thing about world affairs. Nor can you. We live at a time when America is falling due to the rise of China. Its time has come and gone. There was no special blessing from God on America. It just got lucky. It was the only power left standing intact after the Second World War. America also, with Britain, helped to provoke Japan into war by cutting off their access to oil, but fortunately, the ideologues won, and we know now it was a war between democracy and autocracy, between freedom and tyranny.

As soon as the war was over, the colonial powers willingly gave up their possessions to the people for the sake of democracy, right? No. They didn't. The Americans recognized that African Americans were human beings and deserving of citizenship and voting rights. Of course not.

So, if it was not for freedom, why did we fight in the second world war? It was for the rich and powerful, it was for inequality and suffering, it was for white supremacy and a world with the white man at the top. Even today, Christian Fascists crave this world and these old values, and their churches celebrate a world that no longer exists.

Christian Fascists do not follow Jesus Christ

What does all this mean for the church? Christians in America ought not to be surprised at this, but they are often too confused about where the Bible ends, and their nation begins. Covid Hysteria surfed on the fears of the Culture War, the Trump Presidency, the War on Terror, and 9/11. Now, everyone is experiencing the fear of the Ukraine War, the fear of nuclear

Holocaust, the fear of the Culture War, fear of the rise of China.

These are all fears cultivated by the ruling class to function as forms of social control. Fearful people are people who can be controlled, manipulated, and directed. Using foreign policy as a tool for social control and especially fear, fear of others, and fear of our national enemies is one of the most important tools to have been effectively used since 9/11.

The churches thrive on the fear business and are laughing all the way to the bank. This fear machine is what keeps churches going in the West, especially in America. American churches thrive on a diet of fear and sectarian bigotry. They all despise each other as well as hate the latest target in their crusades to cleanse America and bring back the good old days.

These days, I have been listening to some American Christian preachers' rant about Ukraine and Russia. I will not list them by name. I can think of other names I could use to describe them, such as pathological liars, frauds, snake-oil salesmen, con men, crooks, and wolves. They speak to auditoriums full of people. They are incredibly popular. They dominate the airwaves, and their books are bestsellers, and nothing sells better than fear.

The Ukraine War is the best thing for their hip pocket in years. These liars are laughing all the way to the bank with your money. For them, they see Russia as the great enemy of God, in a revived and bizarre rehashing of the old Communist conspiracies. For them, Russia is ushering in the End of Days and will move to destroy Israel with China and Iran as allies. This apparently comes from the ancient Jewish prophecy of Ezekiel chapter 38 and is direct Biblical proof that God is on America's side because America supports Israel. These liars tell us that right back hundreds of years before Christ, Putin was predicted to revolt against the godly and fight against the nation of Israel.

Forget Trump and Biden, the greatest liars are the American Church

I have concluded that not only are these preachers' liars, but their devoted followers, who number into the millions, must be the dumbest people alive. They are bonkers because they have no grasp on their own nation's foreign policy since the 1930s and they don't even bother to read the Bible they hold up and sing about. I don't think they are dumb. They are simply, evil, since they follow their father the devil, who is a liar and the father of lies. I don't believe that these churches seriously care about Ukraine, Israel, or even America. They don't want answers to problems, or solutions to crises. They feed on suffering, they lap it up, they salivate over it during the week looking forward to the next instalment on their fascist bandwagon, they love to hate someone and love to demonize someone, and the last person they want to hear from is God.

Their corrupt leaders are a mirror image of their own depravity. At the heart of every major social and economic and political crisis in America is the church, wheeling and dealing, conniving, and conspiring, dividing, and hating. From the bigoted KKK supporter Billy Sunday to the Anti-Semitic Billy Graham, who opposed the civil rights movement, to the liars who gathered around Trump as their new Messiah, the church in America says little about Jesus Christ, his words, and his life, because Jesus does not fit the narrative of their Culture War, and their love of money, where the church has grown fat with its head in the trough and its bum in the air.

I have already told you about American foreign policy. This is not a conspiracy theory but a fact: America supports nations that hate Israel. Nations are not individuals. There is no global morality, only global interests. America doesn't support Israel; it supports American strategic interests that may or may not align with Israel. If these interests align with Israel, then well and good, but if they do not, then they don't. It is called international relations. This is how superpowers operate. There are no absolutes except national preservation.

America is not the great absolute defender of Israel that many in the church assert. They are blind to what their own nation does to preserve their social and economic well-being. Without access to oil, then these preachers cannot drive their limousines, and without access to Taiwan's semiconductors, they cannot spread lies via their vast internet and TV empires. Thank God for the Pacific fleet and nuclear weapons, after all, without them, these Christian leaders might have to pray to the God they pretend to believe in.

The church does the opposite of Christ

Christians who live in the center of global prosperity are often the blindest, weakest, most corrupt Christians on the planet. Take the abuse of children that has afflicted the church's reputation. Watch these corrupt hypocrites go to the courts to argue that they cannot be sued and that no priest was an employee of their church and therefore their church was exempt from prosecution. Christless, godless semantics, worthy of the worst of the Pharisees, but there was also a big difference, as there were many good men in that ancient sect, unlike today's church.

Oh, they love their property, they love their money, they love their position. Yet Christ tells them clearly – sell all you have and give it to the poor and follow him. If you are in one of these corrupt institutions, sell all your property, give it to the victims of child abuse and follow Christ. To use the words of one of Christ's own enemies: if it is of God, this movement will continue, if it is not, then it will die out, and if it does not, then we will find ourselves fighting God. The reason the Christian Church will not sell its properties is that that is all they have. Beyond their investments and their wealth, and their schools and their properties vital, real faith is absent. But maybe I am wrong, and it is there, deep down, strangled by the love of money. These days, many American Christians cannot tell the difference between Christ and America. Western Christians are completely blind to the world around them, and they cannot tell the difference between their nation and God. This is a curse on American Christianity. Not even the English were mad enough to mix religion and politics to the same depth as they do in America these days.

These Christian Fascists believe that America's enemies are God's enemies, that America is God's nation, and that America is the greatest nation in the history of the world. It is all hubris or as the Teacher would say, it is vanity, all is vanity, a chasing after the wind.

Russia is not the enemy of God

Freedom Matters Today exposes the lies and corruption of the Christian Church and will do so regardless of sect, nationality, or political affiliation. We do it to call to people drowning in the corruption and evil of the contemporary church so they can be free, free of religion, free of fake rituals, and free to make up their own minds.

Russia is not even mentioned in the Bible, not even in Ezekiel 38. It is simply not there. These American preachers have just made it up. They are liars. They want your money and so will lie to your face. They pretend to speak the words of the Holy Spirit and they parrot him and pretend to be him, and they lie to your face.

God speaks through his word, the Bible. If you want to find out what God is saying, read it. Some of these American preachers invent forms of speaking and babble incoherently, claiming that God is speaking through them. They are liars. They make it up or are carried away in fits of hysteria worthy of the caliber of the best Hollywood actors. God speaks clearly, he doesn't babble and whenever angels appear, they speak clearly as well.

Don't you get it, after all these years, they just want your money and power over your lives. They are soul catchers. They want to prevent you from reaching God, seeing God, finding God, and knowing God. They hate

God, they don't believe in him, and they close the door to the kingdom of God, laughing at you, and laughing all the way to the bank. Yes, America does have a claim to fame, there has never been a more corrupt and disgraceful church in the history of the world.

Contemporary Russia is not an ancient state, it dates to the 1990s. These liars read the Bible and they mistranslate it. They read the Bible and they misconstrue it. They read the Bible and they misapply it. These liars say that we wrestle against Russia, that we wrestle against China. This is not in the Bible. These fascists say, *'God bless America.'* But what is the name of this God? Is it the Lord Jesus Christ? Is it Jesus? Really? Where does this come from in the Bible? These liars made this up too.

We can have freedom from fear because of Jesus Christ. These liars never mention him because they do not believe in him. They lie about Christ and make him a footnote to history where America is at the center of God's will. For Christians, Christ is the center of history, the reason for life and faith, and the source of inspiration and hope. Christians will tell you about Jesus and fascists will tell you what to do. Christians will tell you to follow Christ and fascists will tell you whom to hate.

God is not on America's side. He never was and never will be. He is bigger than America and its pitiful ambitions for power. He will still reign as king when all the cities of the US have turned to dust, and all that remains are distant memories. If you are offended by the idea as a Christian than God is bigger than America and that God does not need America to achieve his purposes, then you have no faith and you will die in your sins. God can raise up stones and he can raise the dead to praise his name and live humbly before him, but I do not see humility in Christian nationalism or Christian Fascism.

Following Jesus means listening to him

This Christian Fascism is evil and is a clear and present danger to the people, the nation, and the government of the United States. Imagine Christians in America who followed Jesus instead of the U.S. Constitution, who applied the Sermon on the Mount to their political landscape, or even adopted the attitude of Jesus towards politics.

Imagine a President who has the courage never to invoke God's name again, which is what we call blasphemy. We are told to love others by having the Covid vaccine. Well, Jesus told us to love our enemies, but how do American Christians preach that from the pulpit? They don't. They are too busy hating Russia.

Christians, the antidote to the problems of the world is Jesus. It is not

Donald Trump, the Republican Party, or the fascist Ron DeSantis. It is not even America. God is bigger than the stars and stripes, and his love is like the rainbow that stretches across the sky after the rain. It is always there, and his promises are always true for all people. Jesus does tell us not to worry about the future, not even about tomorrow. We are to keep our minds and our hearts on today, for we only live today. The emphasis of Christ is on the choices we make today, as we seek to follow him.

At *Freedom Matters Today* we try to emphasize personal responsibility in following Christ. We say do not go to church, follow Jesus instead. In other words, if you come to faith, it is your decision to follow, it is not your priest or your pastor or your minister, it is your call, your choice, it is your decision.

In following Jesus, we are urged by him not to worry about tomorrow. We need to return to the Bible, open it, and read it. We will discover that so much we are told in church is simply to keep the fear alive and the money rolling in. But following Jesus offers a different path to those who seek eternal life. As Jesus said in Matthew 6: 25- 34:

"Therefore, I tell you, do not worry about your life, what you will eat or drink; or about your body, what you will wear. Is not life more than food, and the body more than clothes? Look at the birds of the air; they do not sow or reap or store away in barns, and yet your heavenly Father feeds them. Are you not much more valuable than they? Can any one of you by worrying add a single hour to your life?

"And why do you worry about clothes? See how the flowers of the field grow. They do not labor or spin. Yet I tell you that not even Solomon in all his splendor was dressed like one of these. If that is how God clothes the grass of the field, which is here today and tomorrow is thrown into the fire, will he not much more clothe you—you of little faith?

So do not worry, saying, 'What shall we eat?' or 'What shall we drink?' or 'What shall we wear?' For the pagans run after all these things, and your heavenly Father knows that you need them. But seek first his kingdom and his righteousness, and all these things will be given to you as well. Therefore, do not worry about tomorrow, for tomorrow will worry about itself. Each day has enough trouble of its own."

We should worry less, trust God more, and follow Jesus each day.

8   WHEN THE CHURCH GIVES UP ON CHRIST IT RETURNS TO FASCISM

At Freedom Matters Today, we look at freedom from a Christian perspective. This is a minority perspective because the Bible is the last perspective the church wants to present. The last 3 years have seen the worst mass apostasy in the Western church for centuries. Not only did the churches close their doors during Covid, but when they opened, they let the government decide who was allowed in and who was to be excluded. So much for the separation of church and state. The biggest surprise for me was the evangelical churches but then I realized, they have the most to lose financially, and money means more to them than God anyway. Most of these hypocrites still don't see what they did. In Australia, the churches made a fortune from Covid and postponed their inevitable demise for a few more years. They don't need prayer or God or the gospel because they are now on the government payroll.

Then, the coup de grace is the Ukraine conflict and Western hatred for Russia. The churches have said nothing about the persecution of Russian people in the West, the closure of their bank accounts, the end of postal services to Russia, the termination of internet connections, the bullying of their children, the severing of social ties, the expulsion of Russians from employment to name only a few injustices. The only response from these fascists is to say: *'well, they shouldn't support Putin and his regime,'* or *'this is what happens when a nation illegally and immorally invades another nation.'* What punishments did ordinary Americans receive when their government illegally and immorally invaded Afghanistan and Iraq? Nothing. What bank accounts were closed, what postal services, and what internet connections for Americans were severed? None. The churches supported the War on Terror and now they support the American government's proxy war in Ukraine to the hilt. Tell me this, where is this in the scriptures, that the gospel of God is tied to the foreign policy of imperialist power?

I believe that the actions of the church in the West in the last twenty years will result in the oblivion of their witness much like the early Christian gatherings in the first century outlined by John in his Apocalypse. All these gatherings in the first century had a problem and at least they admitted them, but history has shown that they all died out. Churches today, replaced the gatherings and the assemblies and die faster than flies but even when they are at their worst, they never admit their faults, and they feign prayer to God while their backhands are open expecting government money.

If only the church supported the gospel as much as it does foreign policy priorities if only the church preached the gospel as much as it does against gendered minorities if only the church lived the gospel more than it does celebrate dead ritualism. There is no room for God, but that is fine, he is not welcome anywhere.

I visited one of Sydney's largest evangelical churches years ago. It attracts about 1,000 people across a few services or so on the weekend, large by Australian standards, though tiny by global standards. The church is wealthy with a ten-million-dollar budget, lots of pastors, and dozens of volunteers. The head priest wears designer shirts, drives a nice car, and lives in anonymity. At this Sunday evening service, everyone was in tears because they were farewelling a couple who had been with them for years. It was a sad occasion. Their paths were not going to cross again, and they were being sent off in style. I asked the crying person next to me where they were going, was it Africa or China? She looked at me in astonishment and said *'No, they are moving to the 10 am Sunday morning service.'*

Now, in America today, there is a lot of talk about drag queens, transgender kids, and gayness. These minorities have always been with us, except our society is being a little more open about their existence. Nothing new to see here. There is a lot of talk about education and values, and Marxist critical race theory, but there is always a new way of thinking and then the education boards ditch it and pay some young guy millions to come up with a new strategy. Again, nothing new to see here. If you want your kids to have good values, be good parents, and raise them properly.

What I witnessed that Sunday evening at the so-called evangelical church in Sydney was spiritual and moral depravity I have never seen before. This is wickedness, this is evil, and this is symbolic of the devastating cruelty and Satanic character of the church. No normal person would cease fellowship with others because they change church services.

No normal person would weep and cry and lament their passing, moving from what exactly to what exactly? They stay in the same middle-class house, in the same white supremacist town, going to the same coffee shops and same supermarkets, and the same social circle, but what has changed? If you can tell me that something has changed, then you are as lost as they are, you are on the fast track to Hell, and I am sorry, but if you want to defend these people and their dead faith, their fake Christianity, and their fascism, then you are as dead as they are. Only God can raise the dead. When the church gives up on Christ, it returns, like a pig to mud, and a dog to vomit, back to fascism. Every time. Don't go to church, follow Jesus instead.

These reflections end the first series, with God's abiding presence, of the first series of *Freedom Matters Today*. These four books represent the first year of broadcast, blogging, research, and work of a small tax-paying educational service provider committed to proclaiming freedom from a Christian perspective. This is only the beginning. The world needs freedom, and true freedom, which only comes from God. I can do nothing without God's help, and without the work of Christ on the cross, I cannot stand before God, whom I intend to, on the Last Day, with my conscience clear that I did not hesitate to declare the whole counsel of God to all.

I edited this book while with Covid-19, testing positive on Christmas morning, 2022. My hope is that all who have read this book come away with a deeper understanding and appreciation of the Bible, and of the need to follow Jesus. Christian Fascism is not just about the recent resurgence of interest in personalities, policies, and pogroms, but it is about the contest between religion and faith, ritual and relationship, the church and Christ. Now is the time to choose, and the most important question we can ask ourselves is: who is Jesus Christ?

The answer to this question is of eternal significance. Don't go to church, follow Jesus instead. I will continue to put pen to paper until I am taken home to speak of the wonderful work of Jesus Christ on the cross where he took my sins and stood in my place so that I did not have to face God alone or fall when facing Diabolos. We do not wrestle against flesh and blood, and all we meet in life are those to whom the message of the good news of God's grace can be extended. This is a message of God's love, God's sacrifice, and the sure promise of God's freedom.

Remember, freedom matters today because you matter to God.

ABOUT THE AUTHOR

Michael J. Sutton is the founder and CEO of Freedom Matters Today, which looks at freedom from a Christian perspective. He holds a Ph.D. from the University of Sydney (2002), a Master of Divinity from the Australian College of Theology (2017), a Diploma of Bible and Ministry from Moore Theological College (2017), and a First-Class Honours Degree in Economics (Social Sciences), from the University of Sydney, 1995. He spent ten years of his working life in Japan as a lecturer and researcher in international relations and economics in Sendai, Tokyo, and Kyoto. He has published three books:

Freedom from Fascism, A Christian Response to Mass Formation Psychosis

Is God on America's Side?

Is Russia Our Enemy?

All books are published by Hidden Road Publishing.

FREEDOM MATTERS TODAY

Freedom, Matters Today is a tax-paying, educational service provider that looks at freedom from a Christian perspective. We are apolitical and non-sectarian. To date, we have identified six themes: freedom from fascism and tyranny, freedom from fear and despair, freedom from past and prejudice, freedom from guilt and shame, freedom from sin and death, and freedom from war and conflict.

Our slogan is: *'don't go to church, follow Jesus instead.'* Being a Christian is not about going to a building on Sunday but about having a relationship with God. Religion leads to the church, but faith leads to God. God gives us true freedom.

Our books are works of originality and rely upon the arguments and perspectives of the author. They avoid name-dropping or name-calling. There are few, if any, footnotes. If you require verification, Google it. This book is based on our blog and podcast written and broadcast between July 25 and August 31, 2022.

New Testament Greek exegesis reflects the author's academic training but also draws from *Strong's Concordance*, and *BDAG, or A Greek English Lexicon of the New Testament and other Early Christian Literature*, Third Edition, edited by Frederick William Danker, University of Chicago Press, 2000.

For further information about Freedom Matters Today, visit our website at freedommatterstoday.com. We explore faith, life, and what it means to follow Jesus.

Remember, Freedom Matters Today, because you matter to God

www.ingramcontent.com/pod-product-compliance
Lightning Source LLC
Chambersburg PA
CBHW071013040426
42443CB00007B/759